PLAYING THE HARPSICHORD

PLAYING THE
HARPSICHORD

Howard Schott

FABER AND FABER
3 Queen Square
London

First published in 1971
by Faber and Faber Limited
3 Queen Square London WC1
Reprinted 1973
Printed in Great Britain by
Unwin Brothers Limited
The Gresham Press, Old Woking, Surrey, England
All rights reserved

ISBN 0 571 09203 9

CONTENTS

ILLUSTRATIONS

INTRODUCTION

This book is intended to impart the fundamentals of harpsichord playing. It will tell you some basic facts about the instrument, the technique of making music with it, and the vast classical and contemporary repertoire composed for the harpsichord. It will explain the essentials of performance practice and musical style for the classical repertoire. And it will offer guidance for further study through additional reading.

Let me state some assumptions I make about our hypothetical reader. He is familiar with the rudiments of music. He is prepared to look up any unfamiliar word which is not part of the basic vocabulary of musical terms that he already knows. He has some experience in the playing of a keyboard instrument—presumably the piano. If he has not, then it would be well for him to learn his way round a keyboard under the guidance of a teacher before attempting a course of self-instruction based solely on this book. He already has a harpsichord available to him or, if not, he proposes to acquire one.

On this latter point I offer some specific suggestions as well as general guidance. I also have assumed that he is eager to widen his knowledge and will welcome my counsels on further reading.

Most of all, I hope that many pianists, even professionals, may be induced to try their hands at the harpsichord in a serious way, if not in public then at least privately. One of the major obstacles the harpsichord has encountered since the beginning of its modern revival at the end of the nineteenth century has been the reluctance of most pianists to approach it. The example of great pianists like Moscheles who also played publicly on the older instrument in the

mid-nineteenth century, has not often been followed. The idea of
the keyboardist as understood in the time of C. P. E. Bach and
Mozart has slumbered too long. Every serious student of the piano
should have a basic acquaintance with the instrument for which the
keyboard music of Bach, Rameau and Scarlatti was written. It is
surprising indeed that such a grounding has not yet become part of
the conservatory curriculum for pianists.

The revival of continuo playing and the recognition that the
realisation of a figured bass involves far more than a perfunctory
playing of 'correct' four-part harmonies make a familiarity with the
harpsichord in this sense an indispensable part of a conductor's
equipment as well. A performance of any Bach orchestral suite and
many a Haydn symphony without the essential keyboard part has
become unthinkable, far more so in fact than the substitution of
clarinets for high trumpets or the use of outsized performing groups.
The relative availability of instruments for continuo purposes has
increased and will grow still further. Today only a few diehards of
an older generation still cling to the use of a modern concert
grand—closed, of course—strummed by a supernumerary performer
playing from a printed part that contains a harmony exercise
masquerading as a properly realised figured bass.

Finally, I hope that this book will bring joy to many who make
music, the pleasure of playing many works of surpassing beauty on
the instrument for which they were written, and on which they
still sound to fullest effect.

As befits an introduction to the art of harpsichord playing, I must
necessarily stress rules rather than exceptions. In matters of art hardly
any statement one ever makes can be said to be without possibility
of qualification. One may certainly begin with principles bought
ready-made. Their application in practice will necessarily lead to
their modification, perhaps even to their eventual rejection. If the
book serves to start the reader on the right path, its purpose will
have been amply fulfilled.

It is a particular pleasure to record my gratitude to those kind
and generous friends who have helped me in so many ways in its
preparation. Most of all I am indebted to William Dowd of
Cambridge, Massachusetts, who first urged me to undertake it. Dr

William B. Ober and Edwin M. Ripin in New York read the first complete draft and provided the author with many valuable suggestions for improvements. All manner of encouragement and much invaluable practical advice came from many instrument builders, harpsichordists and collectors. To all of these I offer my sincere thanks for all they have contributed.

Oxford, 1971

Reprinting this has offered an opportunity to make a few small changes and corrections. I am indebted to Dr Howard Ferguson and Gustav Leonhardt for valuable suggestions.

Oxford, 1973

I

THE HISTORICAL INSTRUMENT

A harpsichord may be defined as a keyboard instrument with strings sounded by a plucking mechanism. At this point the possibilities of definition are already exhausted, for harpsichords take a variety of forms. I shall use the word in its widest sense as applying to any instrument within that definition.

In the past one referred to the harpsichord proper, shaped like a somewhat narrower and more angular grand pianoforte, the virginal ('virginals', or even 'pair of virginals' used in a singular sense like a 'pair of scissors') with its smaller oblong form, and the spinet, similar to the virginal but of polygonal or 'leg-of-mutton' shape, or even almost triangular. Spinets were almost always, and the virginals were always, instruments with but a single keyboard and only one set of strings, usually sounding at so-called '8-foot pitch', i.e. ordinary pianoforte pitch. The strings of the virginal or spinet were placed laterally, almost parallel to the keyboard, while those of the harpsichord ran the length of the instrument towards its tail. A few virginals and the occasional spinet seem to have been built at 4-foot pitch in earlier times, whence their Italian name of *ottavina*, for they sounded an octave higher than normal pitch.

The names for harpsichord in the principal European languages are of importance to the performer, who will encounter them in the music of their respective countries. In French the harpsichord is known as *le clavecin* while the smaller forms were called *l'épinette* and *le virginale*. In Italian *la spinetta* was the term for the smaller instrument, and the larger was known as *il clavicembalo*, often abbreviated into *il cembalo* or corrupted into *il gravicembalo*.

From the Italian the Germans derived their usual word for

harpsichord, *das Cembalo*, pronounced in the Italian manner. During periodic fits of nationalism, when *Hammerklavier* replaced *Pianoforte*, a German synthetic was substituted, *der Kielflügel*. But *das Spinett* remained the word for the smaller instrument. The generic term *das Clavier*, later spelt *Klavier*, covered all keyboard stringed instruments, not necessarily those of the plucked variety. In the late eighteenth century *das Clavier* usually denoted *das Klavichord*. Today it persists as the term for pianofortes in general and specifically for the upright type as opposed to the grand, known as *der Flügel*, which was another term for harpsichord in the eighteenth century when *Clavier* usually meant a clavichord.

To crown the confusion, in eighteenth-century Spain *el clavicordio* was the term for harpsichord while the clavichord was known as *el manicordio*, the cognates of which were often used in France and Italy in the same sense. A generic word, *la tecla*, literally 'the key' (of an instrument) was used in the sixteenth century and later to refer to both harpsichords and clavichords.

Harpsichords in the 'grand' form were originally merely larger instruments and not necessarily more complex in their construction than virginals or spinets. Only gradually did they come to have two or (most exceptionally) three manuals, and to boast additional sets of strings beyond one or two sounding at 8-foot pitch. These additional sets were normally one sounding at 4-foot pitch and, very exceptionally and quite late, a set giving the octave below, i.e. sounding at 16-foot pitch. In the case of one eighteenth-century German family of builders, the Hass's of Hamburg, we even find a 2-foot set sounding two octaves higher than normal pitch. Thus, from one or more keyboards, the player could play upon from one to three sets of strings in the normal large instrument, and even up to five in the very largest ever built.

The plucking of the strings was accomplished by jacks, thin slips of wood set into vertical upward motion by depressing the keys. Plectra made of quill, or less often of other materials such as leather, plucked the string when the jack rose. These plectra were set in tongues, smaller pieces of wood hinged on pins and placed in a slot cut out near the upper end of the jack. The tongue remained fixed in an upright position during the upward journey of the jack. The plectrum, at a right angle to the jack and the tongue, plucked the string as it passed. To avoid a replucking on the return, the tongue was hinged so as to tip back from the string on the descent. Once the jack had returned to the bottom of its course, a spring restored the tongue to its vertical position. The jacks were carried and aligned by registers, slotted strips of wood, one for each set of jacks.

In modern harpsichords both cowhide and plastic materials are used as plectra in place of the scarce and fragile raven and crow quills. Many makers have also found plastic materials preferable to wood for jacks and tongues. Builders of harpsichords today almost always add a top adjustment screw for regulating the position of the plectrum which controls the intensity of its plucking. A bottom adjustment screw, usually on the jack—occasionally at the end of the key—regulates the length of the jack which controls the timing of the plucking. Attached to the jacks are little pieces of felt or buff leather that serve as dampers. These are also provided with suitable means of adjustment.

As anyone who has ever played a plucked instrument such as a guitar or lute well knows, the point at which a string is plucked has much to do with the timbre of the resulting sound. A string plucked about midway between its points of support, the nut and the bridge, will emphasise the fundamental rather than the partials, producing a rounder, more flutey sound. A string plucked progressively nearer one end of its sounding length tends more and more to yield a pungent, nasal, twangy tone, richer in partials with correspondingly less fundamental. These facts of acoustical life have been fully exploited by harpsichord builders for centuries.

While the plucking points of 4-foot and 16-foot sets of strings are relatively invariable, those of the 8-foot sets can differ more widely. Normally, the 8-foot set controlled by the lower of two manuals or the so-called 'back 8-foot' of a single manual instrument will be plucked closer to the centre of the string. The upper manual or 'front' 8-foot strings will be plucked somewhat closer to the nut. The difference can be compared to the tone of a flute or clarinet on the one hand, and to that of an oboe on the other. In some harpsichords, especially the great English instruments of the eighteenth century, an additional row of jacks, the 'lute stop', was provided for the upper manual of a double harpsichord, sometimes even in a single. These jacks were set to pluck the string very close to the nut, producing a decidedly nasal, twangy sound. To accommodate this additional register a special slot had to be cut diagonally through the wrest plank, the block of wood in which the tuning pins are set.

A more subtle difference in tone-colour results from the choice of plectrum material. While the historical norm was quill, other materials such as leather and metal were occasionally used in former times. Until recently modern makers favoured cowhide almost exclusively, no doubt because of its ready availability and durable qualities. The recent introduction of certain plastic materials, notably Delrin, has brought a revival of quill-type plectra, and thus the reintroduction of a valuable tonal distinction between quilled and leathered registers of jacks in a single instrument. This, too, follows historical precedent, for Pascal Taskin, the famous eighteenth-century French builder, claimed credit for introducing plectra made of *peau de buffle*, a soft leather made of the hide of the Old World buffalo. These yielded a dulcet tone not unlike the sound of early pianofortes, which were already competing with the harpsichord.

Little pads of leather or felt were also often attached to a strip of wood which could be shifted so as to dampen or mute one of the sets of strings. The result was a kind of quasi-pizzicato tone against which the oboe-like sound of the upper 8-foot, for example, could sing most effectively. This device was and is properly termed the 'buff stop' or 'harp stop' in English. The German term *Lautenzug* has unfortunately been imported in a literal but incorrect translation as 'lute stop', a term properly reserved for the register of jacks plucking the string close to the nut. Modern makers usually provide at least one buff stop in every instrument for it adds a useful timbre without requiring additional strings or jacks.

Except in some early Italian instruments, all these devices in harpsichords with multiple sets of strings and jacks could be applied or turned off by levers or stops, more or less like those of an organ. Historically they were actuated by hand and occasionally in late eighteenth-century French and English instruments by knee levers or pedals. Modern instruments have usually had pedals. A recent counter-trend has developed since certain well-known performers have come to prefer hand-stops like those they had used when playing on historical instruments. Hand-stops are usually cheaper and less difficult to build and regulate. It has been said that they offer the advantage that they can be drawn either part-way or fully. In practice this is not really so. In the best modern pedal instruments, however, so-called 'half-hitches', suitable notches in the pedal plate midway between the on and off positions of each register, or special hand levers are available to give a piano or forte voice to each register at the player's choice. By fixing the pedal at the half-hitch or by drawing the piano stop after the pedal for that register has been engaged, the registers are set so that the plectra pluck less strongly than they normally would.

On most old harpsichords with two manuals, the upper keyboard could be coupled to the lower so that the keys of both could be made to play by depressing those of the lower. Historically and in modern hand-stop instruments this is achieved by sliding the upper manual back or the lower manual forward so as to engage pieces of wood called 'coupler dogs' attached to the rear of the lower manual keys which thereupon also operate the corresponding keys of the upper. In pedal instruments the linkage is accomplished similarly by depressing a pedal rather than by pushing or pulling one of the manuals.

In English double harpsichords and some Flemish two-manual instruments there was no coupler. Instead, the normal upper 8-foot jacks were 'dog-legged', that is, they had a downward projection so that the jacks would be lifted by the lower manual keys, too. This still allowed the use of the upper manual as a piano contrast to the forte of the full harpsichord on the lower. But it was musically disadvantageous since no dialogue between two contrasting 8-foot stops was possible. One could only achieve that by using the upper manual lute stop, rather drastically different from the sound of the lower 8-foot. On such instruments pieces like Couperin's *pièces croisées* or the two-keyboard variations in Bach's *Goldberg* set are impracticable. If one tried to use the normal upper 8-foot which played perforce on both manuals, conflicts and overlapping tones would result as if one were performing on a one-manual instrument. If, on the other hand, one used the relatively soft and extremely nasal lute stop above and the louder, flutey lower 8-foot in contrast, the disparity in timbre would be too extreme and the dynamic balance overwhelmingly in favour of the lower manual.

Let us now trace briefly the historical development of the harpsi-chord as it was known to the composers who wrote for it. The earliest instruments we shall be concerned with are mainly Italian harpsichords of the sixteenth century, of which the oldest dated example was signed in 1521. These and indeed almost all Italian harpsichords up to the instrument's decline at the end of the eighteenth century, were single manual instruments with two, or sometimes only one, set of 8-foot strings. Four-foot strings were rare. In many double-strung instruments there was no convenient way to vary the tone by playing alternately on one or both sets. In instruments which did have stops, the knobs were at first located outside the treble end of the case, protruding from the ends of the registers. In other, later instruments the stops were more con-veniently situated above or at the side of the keyboard.

The Italian instruments were either 'grands', oblong virginals or polygonal spinets, some of the latter being ottavinas at 4-foot pitch. They were built of plain wood but then fitted into more elaborate outer cases of painted wood, tooled leather and other luxurious materials, and sometimes even encrusted with jewels. The tone of the instruments, so far as well-restored old examples and modern reconstructions indicate, was quite characteristic with an especially strong third partial, a twelfth above the fundamental, yielding a sound variously described as 'clarinet-like' or 'garlicky'.

While solo harpsichord playing flourished in Italy throughout the sixteenth to eighteenth centuries, the composer-virtuosi con-cerned do not seem to have demanded more complex instruments than the single-manual, two 8-foot register type, basically designed for vocal and instrumental accompaniment. Dr Burney records in the journal of his trip to Italy in 1770 that most households he visited owned only little octave spinets fit merely to accompany a singer. Occasionally he found 'grands' but only of the simpler Italian model so that the one Shudi in Naples and the two Kirckmans in Venice were objects of wonder to the natives of those cities.

By the middle of the sixteenth century the craft of harpsichord building began to flourish in Northern Europe, especially in Flanders where it continued until the late eighteenth century. It was there that the oblong virginal triumphed over the polygonal spinet so far as smaller instruments were concerned. The larger 'grands' as well as the virginals underwent modifications in design which resulted in a sweeter, more silvery sound than that of their Italian forbears. Perhaps this was why large single-manual harpsichords used a 4-foot set of strings as the second register rather than an additional 8-foot set. The less assertive tone of the Flemish 8-foot register with more fundamental and relatively weaker partials needed the brightness of an octave stop.

Flemish virginals were sometimes made in a form known as double virginals, in which a second octave instrument was accommodated, almost kangaroo-fashion, in a space at the opposite side of the case. The *ottavina* could be placed on top of the larger 8-foot pitch virginal, foreshadowing the development of the dynamically contrasted two-manual instruments, since such virginals and octave instruments were coupled together mechanically, giving a combination of 8-foot and 4-foot below, forte, and the 4-foot alone above, piano.

But the development of the two-manual harpsichord in Flanders was also prompted by another motive, that of facilitating transposition. The interval of the fourth, or its inversion the fifth, corresponds to the usual difference in pitch between each two instruments of a family such as the viols or recorders, and to that between the various human voices, too. In an era when pitch varied widely from place to place at different times, practical considerations no doubt led the Ruckers family to make two-manual instruments with the two keyboards apparently a fourth apart in pitch. But the two sets of keys plucked the same strings and were so arranged that if one depressed C on the upper manual, C was indeed sounded. However, if one struck C on the lower manual, G was sounded instead. The need for such instruments must have passed rather quickly. Only one seems to have survived in unaltered form while virtually all the rest were subsequently rebuilt, usually in what became the classic double harpsichord disposition: a lower manual controlling both an 8-foot and a 4-foot register while the upper worked a second 8-foot register. The lower manual registers could be used independently. In addition to combining the two lower manual registers, the player could couple the keyboards so that he might contrast full harpsichord below with the single 8-foot sound above.

Instruments from Italy and Flanders were imported into England at first before makers from those regions set up shops. Large harpsichords were being produced in England by the late sixteenth century, but the oblong virginal was the more popular domestic instrument until it was supplanted by the familiar leg-of-mutton shaped spinet towards the end of the seventeenth century.

In addition to various native builders, such as John Crang, the eighteenth-century English instrument makers include two distinguished immigrants, Kirckman (Kirchmann) from Germany and Shudi (Tschudi) from Switzerland. Upon arriving in London they served apprenticeships with a Flemish builder already established there, one Tabel. Each then opened his own workshop, and produced superb instruments which were in great demand all over Europe as well as in Britain. The smallest were single-manual harpsichords with two 8-foot stops, but to these they often added a buff and a 4-foot, and sometimes, a lute stop. The largest were double harpsichords, richly veneered, with all possible resources except, of course, a coupler, not needed with the dog-legged front 8-foot playable from both manuals. In the last third of the eighteenth century, probably in an attempt to give the harpsichord expressive possibilities like those of the pianoforte, pedal arrangements for changing registers were added and even a Venetian swell device, like an organ's swell box, intended to permit crescendos and diminuendos.

In France the tradition of harpsichord building beginning in the seventeenth century derived largely from the Flemish school. It culminated in the great instruments of the eighteenth century like those built by the Blanchets and their successor, Pascal Taskin, who together with some of the late English makers went on to produce pianofortes as well. While spinets and singles were also built, the emphasis seems always to have been on two-manual instruments. In addition to the basic resources of the double—a quilled 8-foot register on each manual, a quilled 4-foot on the lower, a coupler and possibly a buff stop—Taskin, in rebuilding old Flemish harpsichords, usually added a fourth register of jacks for the lower 8-foot strings, one that was leathered in *peau de buffle*. Some builders used this soft leather in new harpsichords in place of the normal quill plectra of the back 8-foot. French makers devoted much of their time to enlarging old Flemish and earlier French instruments, a matter discussed below with specific reference to keyboard compass. Comparatively few French instruments have survived.

Harpsichord building probably began as early in Germany as it did in Flanders, for we have a dated example from the year 1537. Possibly because of devastation wrought by the Thirty Years War, very few examples of this school have survived from periods earlier than the eighteenth century. While we know of a number of spinets, most of the surviving instruments indicate that the two-manual harpsichord was the prevailing type. In addition to the classic variety of two-manual instrument, the Hass family of builders in Hamburg produced some with a 16-foot stop. Three authentic examples are known and two of these also have a 2-foot stop. One of these instruments is a three-manual harpsichord which is probably the only authentic antique triple extant.

Nonetheless, the courts of Vienna and Berlin saw fit to procure English instruments by Shudi just as German aristocrats in earlier times had purchased Ruckers. The early introduction of the pianoforte in Germany as well as the continued cultivation of the clavichord, even into the nineteenth century, suggest that the harpsichord enjoyed less popularity in Germany than it did in England and France during the eighteenth century.

In Spain the harpsichord kept to its Italian or Mediterranean form in the main: a single-manual instrument with two 8-foot stops. While the double may not have been unknown, at least in imported form, it does not seem to have been cultivated to any great degree. It is therefore to be presumed that Spanish harpsichord music was normally conceived in terms of the single-manual harpsichord.

The matter of compass has been reserved purposely for discussion here because it is complex and somewhat confusing. The earliest keyboards had even smaller compasses than four octaves but we can begin with that range already found in sixteenth-century harpsichords. Most often the four octave instrument was built with a so-called 'C/E short octave'. Although it sounded the four octaves from C to c''', the keyboard appeared to begin at E. However the lowest key sounded C and those used today for F sharp and G sharp gave the low D and E. The F and G keys sounded those notes. Thus the first chromatic note available in the bottom octave was the B flat on the second line of the bass stave. The music of the period took account of this in two ways: composers avoided accidentals in the lowest register, a limitation which was not too troublesome in early times when only a limited range of tonalities was used, and they also exploited the short octave by making use of unusually wide spans. For example, the tenth from low E to G sharp in the top space of the bass stave is beyond the reach of all but abnormally large hands today. It could, nevertheless, be played easily on a short octave instrument because it only involved spanning an octave from low G sharp (sounding E) to the next G sharp. Such unreachable intervals are to be found in the music of the virginalists and even down to the time of Froberger and Fischer.

In later years, when notes down to GG, a fourth below the former limit, were required, builders continued for some time to use a 'G/B short octave'. GG, AA and BB (tuned to BB flat if needed) were produced by the keys we use for BB, C sharp and D sharp. C and D were sounded by the usual keys for those notes. Thus, on such keyboards the first accidental available was the F sharp at the bottom of the bass stave.

Possibly the short octave in its later form was in part the result of rebuilding older four-octave instruments to a wider compass. As noted already, this practice was particularly prevalent in France where Ruckers instruments were successively rebuilt, and preferred up to the end of the harpsichord era. Merely by use of somewhat narrower keys and by extending the keyboards out to the very edges of the instrument, the French rebuilders could enlarge the compass to the full C–c''' range, thus restoring the missing chromatic notes in the bass. Later still, instruments were widened and lengthened to permit their enlargement even to the full five octave compass (FF–f''') introduced in the early eighteenth century. A Ruckers *refait par Blanchet* or by Taskin and given this full extension, called *le grand ravalement*, was highly prized.

Let us now review not only the compass requirements of the principal schools of keyboard composers from the sixteenth to the eighteenth centuries, but also the types of instruments for which they presumably wrote their music.

The Italians counted on their singles with two 8-foot stops and a compass from four octaves (*C–c'''*) to four and a half (*GG–c'''*), usually in short-octave form. Occasionally a top *d'''* was required. Domenico Scarlatti, most of whose sonatas date from his later years in Spain, began writing for the Italian normal compass. In his later works, however, he wrote for five-octave instruments reaching either from *FF* to *f'''* or, alternatively, from *GG* to *g'''*. (The latter compass was peculiar to Spain except that it was used in English spinets and Irish harpsichords.) Rarely does he actually require a two-manual instrument although many sonatas are more easily performed on a double.

German composers wrote mainly for the four-octave compass until the time of Bach and Handel. The earlier composers such as Froberger usually took account of the bass short octave. When they on rare occasions demand notes lower than *C*, it was in terms of the short octave keyboard extending down to *GG*. Handel's music for solo harpsichord requires a compass of *GG* to *d'''*, which is also that of Bach's later works. (The sole *e'''* in the *D* major prelude, BWV 936, was probably inserted for the sake of symmetry by the later copyists on whom we must rely in the absence of the autograph. The *f'''* which occurs in the *Triple Concerto*, BWV 1044, is one of several reasons for questioning its authenticity in its present form.)

Apart from his few pieces actually specifying the two-manual harpsichord, i.e. the *Italian Concerto*, the *French Overture* and the *Goldberg Variations*, Bach rarely requires a double. The same is true of Handel. Little of the music of other German composers appears to demand the second manual. Indeed, the presence of frequent dynamic indications, even limited to mere fortes and pianos, in eighteenth-century German works suggests that they were intended for the clavichord or pianoforte.

The earlier French composers, such as Chambonnières, Louis Couperin and d'Anglebert, composed for an instrument with a compass from GG (bass short octave) to *c'''*, the range of the typical seventeenth-century French harpsichord. Only gradually in the early eighteenth century did composers venture higher, usually no farther than *d''''*. Indeed, in the preludes published in his harpsichord method, *L'Art de Toucher le Clavecin* (1716), François Couperin evidently expected that while all instruments would have low GG, they might not extend beyond *c'''*. He therefore noted that the student could occasionally play the treble part an octave lower than written to avoid *d''''*, possibly missing on his instrument.

Although he wrote a fair number of pieces playable only on a two-manual instrument, Couperin did not exceed the *GG–d'''* compass. (The low *FF* in *La Bandoline*, 5th Ordre, notated as optional, is the sole exception.) He often demanded chromatic notes in the bass which were not available on short-octave instruments.

In his solo pieces Rameau also remained generally within the *GG–d'''* compass, apart from one low *FF* in *Les Cyclopes*. In his late *Pièces de Clavecin en Concert* (1741) alone did he make use of the full *FF–f'''* compass, as did all the late French clavecinistes. Rarely after François Couperin do we find French music playable only on the double harpsichord, but the composers' few surviving registration indications show clearly that they normally composed with it in mind.

In England the virginalists of the late sixteenth and early seventeenth centuries usually wrote for an instrument which did not range above *a''* or below C with a bass short octave. However, there are some pieces which need the missing chromatic tones in the bass and quite a few which descend to *AA*, including such well-known ones as Orlando Gibbons's *The Lord of Salisbury his Pavin* and *Fantazia of Foure Parts* published in *Parthenia* in 1612. By the time of Purcell in the late seventeenth century the *GG–d'''* compass was firmly established. English harpsichords of the eighteenth century were built with a full five octave compass from *FF* to *f'''* (usually without bottom *FF* sharp). A few late instruments even went down to *CC* or up to *c''''*. But composers in England seem generally to have been content with the Purcell range, which was also that of Bach, Handel and Couperin as well.

II

THE MODERN INSTRUMENT

The selection of a modern instrument is not a simple matter. For most of us, one instrument is all that we shall ever own, at least at any given time. There are many builders, each with his own ideas of what should and what can be built as a twentieth-century harpsichord. Some have recently gone to extremes of historicism in violent reaction to some earlier makers of our time who, either out of a mistaken feeling of superiority to the masters of previous centuries, or because of ignorance of historical models, constructed instruments which incorporated many features of the modern piano that do not improve the harpsichord, but rather, tend to debase its character. The best solution to the problem lies between the extremes, I believe. Due respect for the classic principles of harpsichord building and a generally conservative approach do not exclude an intelligent use of modern materials to minimise the difficulties of physical maintenance of the instrument.

The modern revival of the harpsichord dates from about 1882, when a leading piano manufacturer in Paris, Erard, borrowed a 1769 harpsichord from the descendants of Pascal Taskin in order to examine it as a possible prototype for new instruments. Erard did not remain very long in this field. A rival Parisian firm, Pleyel, persisted however, and evolved a first model somewhat closer to a Kirckman than a Taskin. In 1912 they brought out an even larger instrument, with a 16-foot stop, the type of harpsichord created for and made famous by Wanda Landowska who continued to perform and record on it until her death in 1959.

In the 1890s Arnold Dolmetsch in England began to rebuild 'ancient instruments' and to construct new ones, including harpsichords which were played by such pioneer performers as Violet Gordon-Woodhouse. In the course of his wanderings he settled for a while in the United States. For some years Dolmetsch headed a department for harpsichords and clavichords at Chickering & Sons, the piano manufacturers of Boston, and produced a small number of instruments which are prized today by collectors. After a few years of similar efforts at Gaveau's piano firm in Paris, Dolmetsch returned to England in 1913 to establish his workshop at Haslemere in Surrey. The firm that bears his name still produces a wide variety of older types of musical instruments including harpsichords.

In Germany harpsichords were occasionally produced before the 1914 war by piano manufacturers and other builders. Mme. Landowska's classes at the Berlin Hochschule für Musik between 1913 and 1919 produced a whole new generation of players and by 1920 commercial production had already been commenced by a number of firms, such as Neuperts of Bamberg. Today there are many companies and workshops making harpsichords in Germany where the instrument, at least in its smaller forms, has become a favourite means of making music at home. A new generation of craftsmen such as Rainer Schütze of Heidelberg and Martin Skowroneck of Bremen are now emerging in West Germany so that some superb hand-made instruments as well as those produced in larger quantities by firms such as Neupert, Sassmann, Sperrhake and Wittmayer are becoming available. But in East Germany, and indeed in all of Eastern Europe, no maker of significance appears to have emerged, and the few older firms go on producing what are essentially pre-1939 models.

After Dolmetsch's pioneer work in the United States, harpsichords were not produced there again in any numbers until the 1930s when John Challis, a Dolmetsch pupil, returned from Haslemere to establish himself first in his native Michigan, and later in New York City. Since then, a number of builders of superb instruments have come into prominence: William Dowd, Frank Hubbard and Eric Herz in the Boston area, William Hyman in Hoboken, New Jersey, and Rutkowski & Robinette in New York, among others.

In England a tradition founded largely on the Dolmetsch school grew up before 1939 and is still exemplified by the instruments of Robert Goble and the Dolmetsch firm. The harpsichords of Thomas Goff represent a different but related type of consciously modern instrument. Today there are a large number of craftsmen and firms in Britain producing a wide variety of harpsichords. To cite but a few of these, the pure classical tradition is represented by such builders as Derek Adlam, Clayson & Garrett, and David Rubio, while the John Feldberg firm produces instruments in the modern German style and older types as well.

Instruments are also being produced in a number of other countries, notably the Netherlands, France and Switzerland, and it is to be expected that the number of active builders will continue to increase, and the quality of the instruments to improve, too.

The particular instrument one selects is a matter not only of personal finance and preference, but also of what happens to be available. There is no one centre of harpsichord building today. While it is possible to import a harpsichord and many makers, particularly the larger producers, export a considerable number of instruments, it seems wiser, if possible, to choose one made fairly near to where it will be used. Not only will such an instrument have been constructed in the light of first-hand knowledge of the prevailing climatic conditions, but the relative ease of obtaining competent technical assistance and spare parts also weighs heavily in its favour. One would certainly be well-advised to seek out the makers in one's own area first of all, and, in any case, hear and play upon as many instruments as possible. Some piano dealers now stock harpsichords, but a large number of instruments, including a great many of the best quality, are still only to be had on order from individual craftsmen. I have invariably had a cordial welcome whenever I have called upon a harpsichord builder to enquire about his instruments. The builder will usually be happy to indicate where the prospective purchaser can hear or play one of his instruments close to home.

If feasible, a standard of tonal comparison should be sought through hearing or even playing on fine instruments of the past. There are a number of outstanding collections where this may be done. In Britain there are the Benton Fletcher Collection at Fenton

House, Hampstead, and the great Russell Collection recently installed at the University of Edinburgh, as well as collections with untouchable or silent instruments, such as that housed in the Victoria and Albert Museum.

On the Continent many instruments of such great collections as the Paris Conservatoire, the Brussels Conservatoire, the Museums of the History of Music in Copenhagen and Stockholm, the Nuremberg Germanic National Museum, the Deutsches Museum in Munich, the Berlin Musical Instrument Museum, the Kunsthistorisches Museum in Vienna, and others are in playing condition.

In the United States the collection at Yale University, New Haven, is doubtless the richest in playable instruments of highest quality at the present time. The collection of the U.S. National Museum, Smithsonian Institution, in Washington already contains a representative selection of well-restored old harpsichords. Other American museums, such as the Boston Museum of Fine Arts, also have antique harpsichords in working order.

It is sad that some of the richest instrument collections on both sides of the Atlantic remain silent in their glass cases, viewed by their custodians as mere curiosities or, at best, artefacts of purely decorative significance. But as the number of truly qualified restorers is still limited, it is perhaps better that some old instruments should remain unrestored for the time being. In the past, partly from lack of knowledge both of ancient instruments and of modern techniques of conservation, much butchery was perpetrated on antique harpsichords which cannot now be made good.

But beware of accepting at face value gramophone recordings of old harpsichords, even the most recent ones published under the most distinguished auspices. They can often deceive because of room acoustics, electronic witchcraft, and above all the subjective reactions and attitudes of the players and curators concerned with their recording and publication. Valuable as such recordings indubitably are, they are no substitute for the actual experience of hearing a Zenti, a Shudi, a Taskin or a Gräbner.

One basic maxim to be borne in mind is that the musical value of a harpsichord does not necessarily bear a direct relation to its complexity as an instrument. In other words, a good instrument with a single 8-foot stop, resonant and clear in sound from top to bottom, and with a well-made keyboard allowing of a possibility of producing a genuine legato, will be greatly preferable to an inferior harpsichord boasting many registers. To know what a good instrument is presupposes a considerable familiarity with the sound and feel of the harpsichord, which can only be gained by experience. It is well to allow a suitable interval to elapse between the decision to acquire and the actual acquisition of a harpsichord. Unfortunately, the waiting periods for deliveries from many leading makers impose such a requirement on the purchaser in any event. But what if he decides that he is waiting for the wrong instrument? He can usually begin with a smaller harpsichord and then gradually move on to successively larger ones without any great financial loss. The fundamental standard to be kept in mind is a qualitative one. One must not be misled by apparently awesome statistics giving the numbers of combinations obtainable on certain models of harpsichords.

The single factor which weighs most heavily in the cost of a harpsichord is whether it is a one- or two-manual instrument. The larger type is absolutely essential for only two kinds of music:

1. Works such as Couperin's *pièces croisées* and some of the *Goldberg Variations* of Bach where the right and left hand parts constantly cross or even overlap almost entirely; and

2. Pieces which require that the two hands must each simultaneously play at different dynamic levels, such as, for example, Bach's *Italian Concerto*, his *French Overture*, some of the preludes in the *English Suites* and the famous *Fantasy in C minor* (BWV 906).

The first group is of limited importance but the second also takes in many works where it is desirable that the accompaniment should proceed more softly than the cantilena. But, apart from this limitation, the fact of a player's having only one keyboard at his disposal will not hamper him excessively, particularly if the instrument is equipped with pedals or the slightly less convenient knee-levers for making quick changes of registration.

The disposition to be chosen in the case of a one-manual instrument depends in turn on whether it has only one or two or three sets of strings. As already noted, an instrument with only one 8-foot stop is not to be despised, and may be specially suitable for the beginner, provided the small harpsichord has a good tone and an even touch. On a two-string instrument of the Italian type one will usually find two 8-foot stops. Given the sharp attack and relatively quick decay of the sound which characterises such instruments, the lack of a 4-foot stop will not detract from the fullness or brightness of the tutti sound. Indeed, the combination of two 8-foot stops in such instruments usually makes a fuller tone than that of one 8-foot plus a 4-foot, although the latter is also a very popular disposition derived from Flemish models. A three-string single should have two 8-foot stops and a 4-foot. Those rare instruments of that type which have been built with a 16-foot, an 8-foot and a 4-foot represent regrettable errors of tonal judgement in my opinion.

In the case of a double harpsichord a special warning is called for. Modern scholars have established beyond any doubt that a certain harpsichord in Berlin, No. 316 in the Berlin Collection, cannot claim any link with J. S. Bach. It is equally clear that its present disposition (lower manual, 16-foot and 8-foot; upper manual, 8-foot and 4-foot) is the result of alterations made long after its original construction, most likely *c.* 1850. But for many years this instrument was widely accepted as Bach's own and as representative of the type of large harpsichord for which he composed. Thus, virtually all two-manual instruments produced in Central Europe in recent times have been burdened with a disposition which is not found in any authentic old harpsichord.

Still worse, this spurious 'Bach disposition' is musically most impractical. For example, on such instruments one cannot dialogue lower 8-foot and 4-foot against upper 8-foot, a common registration of any movement in concerto grosso form, such as the preludes of Bach's *English Suites*. It is equally out of the question to use this type of double harpsichord in the classical manner for the very purpose for which it was created. Only by fancy footwork can one alternate between full harpsichord and a single 8-foot stop. As simple a piece on a normal historical or modern instrument as the

Echo from Bach's *French Overture* requires constant pedal pumping to be played on these latter-day Central European doubles. All question of the desirability of a 16-foot stop aside, placing the 4-foot register on the upper manual instead of the lower is an obvious error which should not be perpetuated.

As already noted, there is little historical precedent for the addition of the 16-foot register. It is found only in a handful of antique instruments, mainly German ones, and can hardly have been considered as standard equipment even by the latest composers of the eighteenth century. Neither Frederick the Great's Shudis nor Maria Theresa's Shudi, had a 16-foot stop although they did descend in their 8-foot registers to low *CC*. Their length of almost nine feet allowed this exceptional profundity of compass.

Musically speaking, the 16-foot stop has to be used sparingly and with the utmost discretion or else one muddies the contrapuntal lines. The tutti of a well-made instrument without a 16-foot stop in no way lacks fullness of sound. However, many instruments with this additional register can only sound full, especially in the bass, when the 16-foot is engaged. In a movement with a relatively fast-moving bass line, one is faced, therefore, with a choice between inadequacy of sound and tonal confusion.

Next, there is the cost to be considered, not merely in terms of the obviously higher price, but also of what one must give up to have this fourth set of sub-octave strings. A somewhat heavier construction will necessarily result and this seems to lead to a loss of intensity and volume of tone overall. I have heard and played many modern harpsichords as well as antique ones. I have never found one with a 16-foot register that had not sacrificed depth and clarity in the 8-foot basses and general clarity of sound throughout.

Therefore, the disposition of a large instrument, whether single or double, should be based on the classic model; back and front 8-foot stops, and a 4-foot stop. It is advantageous on a two-manual instrument to have a softer 8-foot stop optionally available on the lower, either a second quilled stop or one in a very soft leather like *peau de buffle*. (Some makers can leave space for the subsequent addition of such a second lower 8-foot.) The lute stop is of quite limited musical value and there are ears which do not find it especially agreeable. At least one buff is a desirable addition to the instrument. Some builders always protest at being asked to provide more than one. Others normally fit two buff battens, one for each set of 8-foot strings. Occasionally three are provided in instruments with a 16-foot stop. It is also possible to arrange a single batten on which buff pads are located so that it can be shifted to the right or the left, enabling the player to apply the buff stop to either of the two sets of 8-foot strings.

As a rule one must accept without question the plectrum material —whether it is quill-substitute or leather—that a particular maker uses. This is a matter on which many of them have strong feelings. Some, long committed to the use of leather, still contend that the difference in sound between quill and leather is barely perceptible to the player and not at all to the listener. There is a distinct difference in touch, however. One cannot deny that the leather plectrum can be far more subtly manipulated than the relatively inflexible quill. But the tonal distinction is also far greater than the leather party will admit. The bright, clear sound of quill tends to delineate contrapuntal lines very sharply. What is more, it is far closer to the sound of most antique harpsichords. Properly adjusted modern quill-substitute plectra offer the additional advantage of being virtually indestructible. If anything, rather than wearing out in time as leather does, they tend to harden and have to be trimmed and shaved a bit to reduce the sound after a few years.

But it would be a pity to renounce leather altogether. It has its own beauty as a solo stop and is very lovely as a soft accompaniment register in dialogue with a quilled one. Certainly any 16-foot stop should probably be provided with leather plectra, preferably as soft as possible, as it is a stop which should never obtrude itself.

Whether to have pedals, knee-levers or hand-stops raises questions not only of cash but of convenience and aesthetics. Many makers are willing to provide hand-stops provisionally with later replacement by pedals if desired. There is no doubt that pedals are more convenient, perhaps too much so, for they tempt the player to make registration changes which could not have been contemplated by either composers or performers of the classic period. It will be recalled that the use of pedals in late eighteenth-century English instruments came too late to be considered a historical precedent. Like the use of knee-levers in some very late French harpsichords, pedals were symptomatic of the decline of the classical instrument.

In a single-manual harpsichord, as already pointed out, there is a greater need for quick registration changes as one way of compensating for the lack of a second manual. Pedals are usually to be preferred. But knee-levers work just as well, even if they make the performer appear rather awkward—especially on a concert platform.

Some late eighteenth-century works and virtually all pieces written for harpsichord in our own century require pedal registration. The limitations of a hand-stop instrument in respect of the classical repertoire are trivial, and perhaps even disguised blessings. But there is not the slightest justification for the sanctimonious snobbery about pedals expressed by certain latter-day ascetics among performers and scholars.

Half-hitches on pedals are musically desirable though some makers shun them, claiming they are too troublesome to build and to regulate. There are even some who contend that they cannot be used with quill plectra at all but this must be respectfully but firmly denied. The regulation and voicing of a half-hitch pedal instrument is not unduly difficult and the bit of extra work is well worth the pains. The sounds of individual stops, combinations and even full harpsichord on half-hitch can be ravishing. Although the hand stops used by certain makers for a similar purpose on harpsichords with registration pedals are less convenient to use, they, too, can be regulated to a nicety.

Then we face the question of compass in an all-purpose modern intrument. Clearly only the full range from *FF* to *g'''* will accommodate all music ever written for the classical harpsichord. The Scarlatti and Soler pieces which demand the two top tones are among their very best. The passages in question can hardly ever be adequately rendered by the sudden substitution of a 4-foot register solo. Many makers still refuse to add these two keys at the treble end. But if their obduracy arises from a need to limit the instrument to only sixty-one keys, then it would be preferable to build it with a *GG* to *g'''* compass, as some British and German makers have.

Low *FF* can always be had by tuning down the GG or GG sharp and low *FF* sharp is virtually never demanded.

In addition to the treble extension problem, there is a still more serious one at the bass end. Harpsichords cannot be shortened beyond a certain point without great loss in tonal qualities, especially in the bass. Attempts to compensate for shortness of the case by using wound strings, as one can do with considerable success in a piano, have always worked out poorly.

As a result, the only good harpsichords that can include essential bass notes down to GG or FF must necessarily be of a certain length—surely a good seven feet. Since we live nowadays in more constricted quarters than the people who cultivated the harpsichord in earlier centuries, this poses a serious space problem. It should be remembered, however, that the harpsichord at its widest—that is about 38 inches (97 cm.)—is a good 18 inches (46 cm.) narrower than any piano. Thus, in spite of its length, a harpsichord will not bulk as large in a room as even a small grand.

Compromises have been attempted by a number of makers. Besides the use of the wound bass strings already mentioned, there are short-compass intruments on sale which, even if based on historical models, severely limit the repertoire of those who play upon them! A compass descending only to *C* or even to *AA* means that the player must renounce works which demand the low *GG* or adapt himself to some short octave arrangement of his own devising. It is ironic indeed that at least one factory producer of harpsichords, given to naming each of his models after a famous composer, refers to one of them as 'the Couperin model' although its compass begins at *C*. Thus the preludes composed by Couperin as basic teaching material, which constantly descend to *GG*, cannot be played on this instrument, not to mention the four books of *Pièces de Clavecin*. But then, the same maker's Scarlatti model does not ascend to *g'''* either. If any compromise in the matter of compass should be required, *GG* to *d'''* would seem the only reasonable one.

The purchase of a second-hand instrument, often at a considerable saving in money and delivery time, may now and again be possible from harpsichord builders or owners. The risks of such a transaction are obvious. Particular dangers attach to instruments whose makers are so far away that details of provenance and maintenance cannot be verified. Buying a previously-owned instrument from a builder who is not necessarily the same person as the builder who made it, is less uncertain. If he is responsible, the instrument will have been put into proper condition before being resold.

Finally, a word is required concerning 'do-it-yourself' harpsichord building, a matter in which I have had no direct personal experience. For some years past, particularly in the United States, instruments in kit form have been offered by a number of builders at comparatively low cost. Some of these, when constructed with the best of materials and the greatest of care and skill, have proved to be excellent. Others seem faulty in design to the point where no amount of pains taken over their construction can improve their basically unmusical quality. It is obvious that only a person who is already quite familiar with the techniques of working with wood ought to attempt such a complex project. Before undertaking the building of a more elaborate instrument, he might do well to attempt a simple one which could be disposed of and replaced later on.

One advantage to be gained from the experience, no doubt, is that the burdens of harpsichord maintenance will not weigh so heavily on the amateur builder, even if he ultimately discards it for one made by a professional. What is more, he will be less easily deceived by bad workmanship and the readier to appreciate good. Occasionally a harpsichord or piano technician may be willing to build a kit instrument on commission, but the saving in cost sometimes diminishes at that point to such a degree that it may be wiser to settle for an instrument that carries the guarantee of a reputable maker. However, there are also specialists who have built up a flourishing custom by constructing kits to order. Some of the results recently attained by these middlemen of the craft are very impressive indeed.

III

THE MUSIC OF THE HARPSICHORD

The repertoire of music composed for the harpsichord is vast. Over four centuries of enormous productivity lie between the date of the earliest pieces and 1750. After that date composers wrote primarily for the pianoforte and, in Germany and Scandinavia, for the large eighteenth-century clavichord, too. Following a lapse of more than one hundred and fifty years, this repertoire has begun to expand again in our own century.

Until recently most harpsichordists tended to concentrate their attention on the great composers of the eighteenth century, Bach, Couperin, Handel, Rameau and Scarlatti, with only an occasional backward glance to the sixteenth- and seventeenth-century masters. Yet, much of the finest music for harpsichord dates from those earlier centuries and a principal purpose of the present survey of the harpsichord repertoire is to call attention to some of these neglected masterpieces.

In a brief survey one can only hope to point out the major peaks, the harpsichord music which on no account should be neglected by players of the instrument. Some of this music was shared by the harpsichord with other keyboard instruments—the clavichord and the organ, and even the lute and its relatives. The earlier composers, especially, tended not to specify a single keyboard instrument for the performance of their works and printed music was almost invariably described on its title page as suitable for every type of keyboard. Even pedal parts that would seem to call for the organ, were often stated to be optional so as to permit performances of the piece on instruments with only manual keyboards. The rare dynamic indications were not such as to exclude the harpsichord but can be interpreted as suggesting the use of a two-manual instrument.

It is not until after the first third of the eighteenth century that keyboard music begins to appear with frequent and varied dynamic indications which point clearly to the pianoforte or the clavichord, especially in Germany. The changing aesthetic—the replacement of 'terrace' dynamics by crescendo and diminuendo gradations—was in part responsible for the development of the late harpsichords with knee-lever or pedal registration changes, and even Venetian swells. On our modern instruments with registration pedals we can no doubt 'fake' our way even through post-1750 keyboard music which late eighteenth-century harpsichordists certainly played; nevertheless the true harpsichord literature is so large that there is no need to force its bounds. Those late works are better left to the clavichord and the pianoforte.

THE SIXTEENTH CENTURY

True antiquarians can turn back to an English manuscript, the Robertsbridge Codex, dated by some scholars as early as 1320, and to a slightly later and much larger Italian collection, the Faenza Codex. The fifteenth-century manuscript sources are still richer and more varied in content, but only manuscripts of German origin have survived. These earliest pieces are not especially idiomatic. One can easily imagine performing them on almost any combination of instruments.

By the sixteenth century the flood gates have opened wide. Even more impressive than the quantity of pieces is their idiomatic quality. The keyboard feeling of Hugh Aston's *Hornpype* and its nine anonymous companion pieces in a British Museum manuscript of about 1520 makes them play and sound like genuine harpsichord music. Two of them, *My Lady Careys Dompe* and *The Short Mesure off My Lady Wynkfylds Rownde*, in spite of their droll titles offer splendid examples of the spirited dance music of the time presented in versions designed for keyboard performance.

The sixteenth century offers a broad range of music for the

harpsichord. There are many pieces conceived in forms especially suited to keyboards. The prelude, for instance, was doubtless developed as just that—an instrumental introduction to a textually-based vocal work such as a motet or chanson, and designed to set the mood for what was to follow. The toccata, a richer, more expansive form, not only features the chordal patterns and flowing lines and roulades of the prelude, but adds imitative passages worked out in the manner of vocal polyphony. This type of toccata persists down through the centuries to the toccatas of Bach, after which the form degenerated into mere display pieces for the virtuoso.

Much sixteenth-century keyboard music is directly derived from the prevalent secular and sacred vocal forms: the madrigal, the chanson and the motet. The top voice of the free adaptations of vocal pieces is usually embellished and embroidered in smaller note values—'coloured' as it was said. Whether this was done in imitation of the free ornamentation practised by singers or for the purpose of enlivening the sound of the keyboard instrument we cannot say for certain.

The ricercar, usually based on a fragment of liturgical music, is a sectional form in which the voices answer one another in contrapuntal imitation with the 'colouring' largely confined to the uppermost part. The sections are often divided by brief interludes based on chord progressions. In its pristine pattern the ricercar is probably more suited to the organ than to the harpsichord. But in its related forms, usually known as fantasies or capriccios, with their more idiomatic working out of the parts, such music often comes vividly to life on the harpsichord, particularly if played with great freedom and dash—or on occasion with virtuoso abandon.

The specific harpsichord pieces in this genre are usually derived from the secular vocal forms of the sixteenth century's 'Golden Age' of polyphony, and variously termed chanson, canzona, frottola and madrigal. It is perhaps an exaggeration to compare such transcriptions, also performed on the chamber organ, clavichord and lute, with modern jazz piano versions of well-known tunes. But the parallel should be kept in mind if only to avoid a staid and rigid type of performance, lethal to older music. Certainly those harpsichordists who have sung some of the vocal prototypes of these *canzone da sonar* (i.e. songs to be played) enjoy an advantage over those who have not.

A few suggestions on performance will be helpful. The openings of many of these pieces—great white notes suggesting the slowest of tempi—are quite deceptive. Solid chords should be arpeggiated or broken up into figured patterns at times. Look and see what happens later on and take your tempo at the beginning with an eye on subsequent passages with the smallest note values. Do not hesitate to point up an imitation by introducing an ornament (trill, mordent or even a turn) on an important note or two, provided you can do so with equal grace in each part. Dwell on the big cadences which mark off the main sections of the piece, ornamenting them if possible with a trill or turn in the upper voice, as is sometimes, though not always, indicated in the original text.

Most accessible of all to the modern harpsichordist will be the dance pieces of the sixteenth century. Here the harpsichord early found its place not only as a solo instrument but in the ensemble music of the time as well. And what a rich variety of dances there are: peasant dances, like the morris dance (morisco); gliding dances like the basse danse; and leaping dances like the saltarello. Very often the dances were performed in pairs, a grouping which ultimately developed into the dance suite. Commonly, a slower dance in duple time, such as the pavan and passamezzo, was followed by a quicker one, like the galliard or coranto, in triple metre.

In the sixteenth century these pieces in the main still represented the pure form of the dance. They were conceived as music for dancing, and not as idealised or stylised instrumental forms. It is precisely the difference we see between a piano arrangement of a Viennese waltz, and the highly refined keyboard waltzes of Chopin and Brahms. So, too, a typical simple sixteenth-century pavan set for harpsichord differs from one of the mighty expansions of the form in the works of Byrd, Bull or Gibbons of the late sixteenth and early seventeenth century.

In the sixteenth-century dances it is well to emphasise the basic dance rhythm to a still greater degree than in the later stylised versions. While they were originally played on simpler instruments, spinets with one 8-foot register or harpsichords with two, some colouring through registration can legitimately be introduced. After all, not all harpsichords, or even those with similar specifications, sound alike; moreover, ensemble performance was also contemplated. For example, one can play the upper part, the tune, of a repeated section an octave higher than the first time round, either making use of a 4-foot stop or moving the part up an octave if the compass permits. The accompaniment may possibly sound to advantage played on a buff stop. A contrasting 8-foot, perhaps a lute stop, can also be used for contrast. What should be avoided is the indiscriminate piling up of register upon register, and changes of registration within the sections.

In the slower dances, especially, free ornamentation can be introduced to emphasise the big cadences and vary the repeats. In the faster ones it will take more skill to do this gracefully in the brisk tempos required. Models of such ornamentation in written-out form will be found in a number of old dances, for instance those in the 1551 Venetian collection called *Intabolatura Nova di Balli*, available in modern reprints. One form of ornamentation frequently employed—a turn of an even four notes over the leading note at a cadence—can usually be managed in all but the quickest of dances.

Ex. 1 Dalza, Pavana alla Veneziana

Special mention must be made of one of the genuinely great keyboardists of the sixteenth century, the court organist of Philip II of Spain, Antonio de Cabezón. Both highly intimate and personal feelings and the grandeur of the Spanish sixteenth century, *el Siglo de Oro*, find musical expression in the works of this blind musician who accompanied his royal master throughout the Continent and to England, too. His pieces suitable for harpsichord fall into two main groups: the *tiento*, a sort of prelude or, in its more extended examples, a ricercar in imitative style; and sets of variations on folk tunes. Cabezón is one of the most praised and least played of early keyboard composers, probably because in his case the gap between the written notes and the intended performance seems specially large. The intrinsic beauties of his music are such that even a straightforward reading, literal and unembellished, of many pieces can be very satisfying. A few such pieces particularly suited to introducing performer and listener to Cabezón's style are the variations on *El canto llano del Caballero*, the *Pavana Italiana*, the *Gallarda Milanesa*, and the different sets of variations on the folksong, *Guardame las Vacas*. You may find some of the lute or vihuela pieces of Luis Milán and Mudarra simpler and more approachable than the more austere style of Cabezón and his school.

THE SEVENTEENTH CENTURY

While much of the keyboard music of the sixteenth century was to a considerable extent shared by the harpsichord with the clavichord and the organ, that of the seventeenth seems to take on a more clearly defined instrumental quality, although still without absolute separation of the repertoires of the three types of keyboard. The art of harpsichord building had made giant strides in the latter part of the sixteenth century, and by the dawn of the seventeenth, the great Italian makers and the Ruckers dynasty in Antwerp were at their zenith. The interaction of stylistic and instrumental development was of vital importance to the burgeoning of the harpsichord repertoire that occurred after about 1580. Which was cause and which effect need not concern us here.

The separation of harpsichord music from the general mass of keyboard writing is somewhat clearer in the case of France and England. Composers in Italy, Germany and the Low Countries still continued to write in a less clear-cut style, somewhat ambiguously placed between harpsichord and organ music. National styles, too, became more pronounced in the seventeenth century—in spite of the fact that composer-performers now travelled far more widely than ever.

From the standpoint of form, the seventeenth century continued on the paths established in earlier times. In the realm of so-called absolute music, the fantasy, capriccio, toccata, canzona and ricercar —now sometimes referred to by its modern name of fugue—still held sway. On the Continent the fantasy was less organised, more fantastic if you will, than in the similarly named, tightly woven pieces of that name so popular in England, written for the harpsichord and the consort of viols. For example, Orlando Gibbon's masterly *Fantazia of Foure Parts* in *Parthenia*, published in 1612, might well have been entitled a ricercar or capriccio if an Italian had been its author.

Whatever technical distinctions scholars may draw and redraw periodically among various 'forms' such as ricercars, canzonas and capriccios, the fact is that from our twentieth-century point of view, we see them as precursors of the fugue. This form, even in its last flowering in eighteenth-century Germany, sometimes used themes akin to folksongs as well as fragments of wellworn material, purely abstract 'tags' and bits of old liturgical music.

The dance was by no means forgotten but some of the forms and rhythms changed. In addition to the pavan and galliard, which continued in favour longer in their stylised keyboard versions than as dances, we now find all four elements of the classical dance suite, the allemande, courante, sarabande and gigue, as well as a variety of others, notably the minuet and the chaconne.

The grouping of dances into suites of more than a mere pair which began towards the middle of the seventeenth century is said to derive from the practice of lutenists, the tuning of whose instruments varied, depending on the tonality in which they were playing. A whole series of dances would be put together for performances in a single key, thus avoiding the need for frequent retuning. The whole interrelationship of lute and keyboard music is of great fascination. Many of the thinner-textured though highly complex lute versions of music which was simultaneously or later given a keyboard treatment are very illuminating, and well worth playing on the harpsichord. They were actually transcribed into keyboard notation at the time.

The relatively brief span of the English virginalists, from the last quarter of the sixteenth century to the second quarter of the seventeenth is as puzzling as their sudden rise. There was an old tradition of keyboard music in Britain, as we have seen, going back to its very origins. But the music of such collections as *The Mulliner Book* (between 1560 and 1580) gives only a bare hint of the miracles to come a few years later. It was in England that harpsichord music first appeared to take a separate and independent path and go its own way, no longer tied to organ and vocal music.

The two most famous of the many collections of the time, present the world of the virginalists in macrocosm and microcosm. The three hundred or so pieces of the *Fitzwilliam Virginal Book*, a manuscript of *c.* 1610, and the 21 pieces of *Parthenia*, published in 1612, between them offer a generous and representative selection of the total output of the school, amounting in all to more than seven hundred pieces. Many of the Fitzwilliam pieces and probably some in *Parthenia*, too, must be dated years earlier. The larger collection also contains a number of pieces by foreign composers, such as Giovanni Picchi and Jan Pieterszoon Sweelinck, as well as keyboard settings by English composers of Flemish, Italian and French vocal works.

Regardless of the actual form of particular pieces, the dominant tendency pervading all virginal music seems to be the variation principle known as diminution, which involves the use of smaller and smaller note values as the piece progresses. Not only is this true of the variations on folk and hymn tunes, but every reprise of almost all the dance tunes seems to have been similarly varied. Some composers actually added new, varied versions that are separate pieces in themselves. Only a relatively few, short and uncomplicated dances were left in the plain, unadorned format of earlier times. The *Fitzwilliam Virginal Book* alone contains three versions by Byrd, Morley and Giles Farnaby of John Dowland's famous pavan, *Lachrymae*, which also exists in many other virginal settings.

There were some exceptions, notably the preludes which are worked out more fully but on the same formal lines as those of the sixteenth century. Still, the virginal, particularly in its usual limited sense of a small, oblong harpsichord, was an instrument that scored its musical points in a voluble way, the tone generally having a pronounced pluck and a relatively quick decay. The basic tendency was to write many notes following each other in quick succession. Even those pieces which begin slowly and quietly soon grow by diminution into strings of passages, scales, and sequences of all sorts and are richly decorated with ornament signs as well.

The pieces of the older generation, that of William Byrd (1542–1623), a kind of lyric poet among the virginal composers, can sometimes prove very difficult technically. But they do not quite reach the extremes of virtuosity attained in the next generation, dominated by John Bull (1563–1628), who is termed by some 'the Liszt of the virginal'. The third and last group is characterised mainly by the romanticism of its leading figure, Orlando Gibbons (1582–1625). The tradition of the virginalists came to an end with the death of the last of them, Thomas Tomkins, in 1656.

Two of the virginalists took refuge in the Low Countries—Peter Philips in about 1582 and John Bull in 1613. They are therefore seen as two direct links between the English virginalists and the Netherlandish keyboard school centring round Jan Pieterszoon Sweelinck (1562–1621). Four of his pieces, it will be recalled, were included in the Fitzwilliam collection while Sweelinck's other works also illustrate the link, for they include a varied version of a pavan by Philips as well as a transcription of John Dowland's *Lachrymae* pavan. Bull, in a piece dated 15th December, 1621, paid tribute to Sweelinck's memory by composing a fantasia on one of the Dutch composer's fugue subjects.

The artistic interchange between England and the Low Countries constituted only one of the various influences that made themselves felt in the musical life of the Netherlands. Sweelinck never left his homeland, yet he was able to benefit from Italian, French and even Spanish artistic currents. How much of his keyboard output is harpsichord music proper may be debated. The fantasies and toccatas, full of contrapuntal ingenuities reminiscent of Merulo and the Gabrielis, often succeed well on the harpsichord. They were more likely to have been intended for the organ which the composer played daily in concerts in the Oude Kerk in Amsterdam. But his variations on well-known songs and dance tunes, clearly for harpsichord, speak in a much more English idiom—except for a few characteristic figures which recall Frescobaldi, with whom

Sweelinck became personally acquainted. Some of the same tunes were also treated by the virginalists.

Sweelinck's variations are melodic with the theme usually in the top voice, no matter which part happens to be embroidered at a particular moment. These pieces are most heartily recommended for their musical qualities and instrumental allure. The very moving and technically demanding set of variations on *Mein junges Leben hat ein End* should be in the repertoire of every harpsichordist. Somewhat simpler technically and quite delightful to play are those on the *Ballo del Granduca*, a dance tune said to have been composed by Emilio Cavalieri in 1589 for a Medici wedding feast in Florence.

We next turn back to Italy, one of the focal points of our attention during the sixteenth century, but it is to Rome rather than Venice. Although Girolamo Frescobaldi (1583–1643) was a native of Ferrara, it was in Rome that he spent his active life, first as organist of Santa Maria in Trastevere, then from 1608 at St Peter's. Just before this final appointment, Frescobaldi visited the Netherlands, spending about a year in Brussels and Antwerp. It is virtually certain that he must have had personal contact with Sweelinck and known the Northern European keyboard-music tradition, both Continental and British, at first hand.

Frescobaldi's music for keyboard lends itself extremely well on the whole to performance on the harpsichord. Except for a few toccatas with obbligato pedal parts, and for the *Fiori Musicali*, a collection of organ pieces specifically intended for liturgical use, the greatest part of his music succeeds admirably on the plucked strings of the harpsichord. It includes dance pieces first of all: courantes, chaconnes, passacaglias, galliards and others. And there are also sets of variations (or *partite*) on well-known tunes and ground basses of the day, and a large number of contrapuntal pieces: ricercars, canzonas and capriccios, as well as toccatas.

Quite a few of Frescobaldi's pieces are immediately accessible, for example, the variations on *La Frescobalda*—very familiar in transcriptions for guitar—and the courantes. But the contrapuntal works, and particularly the toccatas, require deep study. One must steep oneself in the style and, above all, learn to play them with unusual freedom. Once more we sense that the most important part of the music is not in the printed notes. Fortunately Frescobaldi left rather specific directions for performing his music in his prefaces. In substance what he tells us is that we must play with considerable freedom, even rubato, making retardations at the cadences, and articulating runs in a special manner. In particular, he directs us to make the performance of even the most virtuoso passages both meaningful and expressive. His directions bear, surely, not only on his own music but also on that of many late sixteenth- and early seventeenth-century works in similar forms. Frescobaldi was a contemporary of Monteverdi's, and the romantic spirit was not born in 1800!

Germany in the early seventeenth century did not boast a master of the harpsichord of the stature of a Bull, Sweelinck or Frescobaldi. The most worthy of her keyboard composers of the period was certainly Samuel Scheidt (1587–1654). After study with Sweelinck in Amsterdam, Scheidt spent his life as an organist in Halle during the troubled times of the Thirty Years War. In addition to some variations of his own incorporated (possibly only by copyists) in works composed by Sweelinck, Scheidt's harpsichord works comprise sets of variations and dance movements. Some were published in 1624 in his *Tabulatura Nova*, a collection principally of organ pieces. Others have come down to us in manuscripts of the period. Scheidt's variations show a highly developed architectural sense, continuing the tradition of the virginalists as passed on through Sweelinck and also incorporating occasional Italian traits.

It is in France especially that we find a flowering of harpsichord music at this time, centring first of all on the figure of Jacques Champion de Chambonnières (1602–1672). Descended from a line of court musicians, Chambonnières succeeded to his father's post as harpsichordist to Louis XIII and continued in that capacity into the reign of Louis XIV. But, suddenly, for unknown reasons, he fell abruptly from favour in 1662, dying about ten years later in relative obscurity. Chambonnières is in every sense the founding father of the great French school, the first of the clavecinistes—a line which continued up to Rameau's last harpsichord piece, *La Dauphine* (1747), and even beyond into the time of Duphly.

Chambonnières's music derived totally from the dance. One looks

1. Harpsichord by Andreas Ruckers the Younger, Antwerp, 1637

*Dr. Ulrich Rück Collection of Old Musical Instruments
in the Germanische Nationalmuseum, Nuremberg*

2. Virginal by Thomas White, London, 1642

Victoria and Albert Museum, London

in vain for ricercars, fugues, canzonas, toccatas or fantasias. Except in the limited sense of the 'double', there are no variations, either. The form is uniformly binary except for the solemn pavans, still in the traditional three sections, and the rondeau-type pieces, including some glorious chaconnes. Rhythms dominate, especially the ambiguous pulse of the French courante, which vacillates between three times two beats and two times three, never quite making up its mind. Not only the dance suite form with its uniform tonality but also the texture and the lay of the pieces point strongly to the influence of the lutenists of France. The single tonality of the suite is refreshed by the alternation of rhythms and tempos: allemande and courante, sarabande, pavan and galliard, gigue and chaconne. The uniformity of the binary form is relieved as well by the practice of varying the reprises of each section. We have a number of authentic doubles by Chambonnières and other composers for his pieces. In his two published books of pieces, Chambonnières makes extensive use of signs for the ornaments so beloved of the clavecinistes. He has been reproached for being precious but to our ears his music epitomises the rationality, the grandeur, the elegance of his age. These are not all pieces to be tinkled on a spinet. Many of them, such as the famous Chaconne in F (No. 116) and the pavan entitled in lutenist fashion, *L'Entretien des Dieux* (No. 24), are in the grand baroque manner.

Johann Jakob Froberger (1616–1667), a native of the Stuttgart region, probably travelled more than any other musician of his time. Organist for some years at the Imperial Court in Vienna, he visited Italy, Northern Germany, the Low Countries, England and France, learning, absorbing and expanding his artistic horizons in each country. His four years in Rome, made possible by a grant from the Emperor, included study with Frescobaldi, whose stylistic influence is evident in his ricercars, toccatas, canzonas and capriccios. Nonetheless they have their own character and cannot be called derivative in any pejorative sense. Many, or even most, of these contrapuntal pieces are quite well-suited to the harpsichord. But it is in the suites that Froberger speaks most eloquently and personally to us. Indeed, at times he appears as a kind of seventeenth-century German expressionist, writing 'blues' for harpsichord of an unparalleled expressive intensity. (See, for example, the allemande of Suite XX in *D* major, Froberger's *Memento Mori*.)

In his use of the suite form Froberger was a pioneer in Germany. One of his most famous suites, no. VI, *Auff die Mayerin*, is actually a set of variations on a folk tune, with several movements in dance rhythms. Some of the allemandes of the suites bear titles. They are invariably sad in tone: e.g. *Plainte faite a Londres pour passer la Melancholie* (Suite XXX), and *Lamento sopra la dolorosa perdita della Real M^sta di Ferdinando IV, Rè de Romani, etc.* (Suite XII). Equally striking are the *Tombeau fait à Paris sur la mort de Monsieur Blancheroche* —Louis Couperin spelt the name of the deceased correctly in his elegy on the same unhappy event—and a lament for Emperor Ferdinand III dated 1657.

At mid-century we pause and look back at the great names and works of the first seventy years of the seventeenth century—the virginalists, Sweelinck, Frescobaldi, Scheidt and Chambonnières. What variety, what a rich field for exploration they present to the harpsichordist! Yet up till now their music has been played far less than it deserves.

The works of such seventeenth-century English worthies as Matthew Locke, Jeremiah Clarke, John Blow and William Croft need no extended discussion. In a brief survey they can figure only as contemporaries of Henry Purcell (1658–1695). A slender volume containing eight suites and some two score single pieces, many transcribed from his stage works, are all that Purcell has given us for the harpsichord. Among the individual pieces it is the grounds which stand out. This form comprises variations over a persistent bass on a motive in the soprano part. The motive is repeated between the variations in the manner of the French *chaconne en rondeau*. The suites are short, and often prefaced by a prelude in contrapuntal or even concerto style. They lack the gigue which was not yet a standard element and was often lacking in the suites of Chambonnières and Froberger, too. Purcell fills out his suites with hornpipes, airs and minuets. The writing is often deceptively simple so that free ornamentation, particularly in the repeats, is appropriate except in those rare cases, like the filigree Almand of the seventh suite in *D* minor, where the line is already almost too richly decorated.

Of the many Italians at work on keyboard music in the latter half of the seventeenth century, Michelangelo Rossi (died after 1670), Bernardo Pasquini (1637–1710) and Alessandro Scarlatti (1660–1725) stand out against a musical background dominated by myriad works for strings and voices. Rossi's surviving keyboard works, in part for organ, have only recently been published accurately and in full. A few dance pieces and variations in the Frescobaldi tradition and fourteen toccatas make up this small volume.

Bernardo Pasquini's pieces offer a wider range of styles and forms. In addition to variations, toccatas, canzonas, dances, suites and airs, Pasquini was amongst the first to compose sonatas—not in the style of the late sonata writers certainly, but already showing the formal traits taken up and developed so fully by the younger Scarlatti. Pasquini must have possessed a formidable keyboard technique. His most popular piece, the famous *Toccata con lo Scherzo del Cucco*, requires a capacity to play extended trills and simultaneous counterpoints to it in the same hand that is hardly matched by any keyboard writing before Beethoven. The suites open with the usual allemande —courante pairing, but omit the sarabande before the final Italian jig. Here again we see that the classical suite form was rather less standardised than one is led to believe by late examples and textbook rules.

Alessandro Scarlatti's importance as a keyboard writer does not equal his importance as a composer of operas and cantatas. Indeed, we might go so far as to say that his major contribution to keyboard music was the siring of his illustrious son, Domenico. But it is rewarding to gain an acquaintance with the father's toccatas and other pieces, including those virtually endless variations on *La Folia*, a theme famous from its treatment by Corelli. There is one toccata in G major published in the composer's lifetime with authentic fingerings that are of interest in suggesting ways to articulate the long concatenations of notes in much early keyboard writing, so often the despair of performers.

Germany suffered less than Italy from the competition of the violin, which brought about some decline in the importance of keyboard music there during the latter half of the seventeenth century. German organists who kept the keyboard traditions alive

were also active on the secular side. Works based on chorale tunes
and fugues on fragments of plain chant, like some of Pachelbel's,
could be interpreted effectively on stringed keyboards. Unlike in
France and Italy where the harpsichord reigned almost unchallenged,
Germany's composers continued to write for both harpsichord and
clavichord. It is often difficult to assign specific compositions to one
or the other instrument; fortunately, most succeed quite well on
both.

Two of the three streams of influence that flow together in late
seventeenth-century German keyboard music are familiar. One is
clearly Italian, the tradition summed up in Frescobaldi. The other
can properly be termed 'North Sea', for it takes in more than the
Netherlands and Sweelinck's orbit, and includes the Hamburg
organists as well. To these was added a new third current flowing
from the French style created by Lully—that Florentine who
became the most French of opera composers—and by the orchestral
suite writers, the lutenists and the earliest generation of clavecinistes.
(The way is being prepared for the final summation of all baroque
styles in Bach and Handel.)

Passing quickly over Georg Muffat (c. 1645–1704)—a pupil of
both Pasquini and Lully—Alessandro Poglietti, an Italian active in
Vienna until killed by the Tartars in 1683, and Johann Kaspar Kerll
(1627–1693), a pupil of Carissimi in Rome, we come to Johann
Pachelbel (1653–1706), who left a large number of keyboard works.
The ninety-four fugues on the Magnificat are generally considered
as organ music. However at least two of them were unforgettable
as played by Landowska on the harpsichord. The airs and variations,
the suites in the French manner, and such single pieces as the glorious
chaconne in F minor, are Pachelbel's great legacy to the harpsichordist. The touching and utterly simple variations on the chorale
tune *Werde munter mein Gemüthe*, freely translatable as 'Cheer up,
my soul', come from a collection entitled *Musikalische Sterbensge-
danken* (or Musical Thoughts on Death), a grim example of the
German pietistic style of the time. The sets of variations in the
Hexachordum Apollinis collection are equally rewarding to play.

Quite as commonly underestimated as Johann Pachelbel is Johann
Kasper Ferdinand Fischer (c. 1665–1746), who spent his active life

as court conductor to the Grand Duke of Baden. We need not linger over his preludes and fugues or ricercars, but the seventeen suites are quite another matter. They are far more than imitations of the French dances which were the rage at the court of every German princeling. The preludes are often quite extended—some in toccata form and others in French overture style—but many are of a more modest cut. Fischer's sense of proportion in his suites is sometimes strange. The uniquely grand passacaglia which ends the last suite in *D* minor is itself half as long as all the preceding movements put together. But this stirring passacaglia can be played alone, as can some free groupings of dances from the suites. French performing style, with its overdotting, unequal notes and occasional *petites reprises* (a second repeat of the final bars of the latter half of a dance), would seem appropriate, indeed essential for playing Fischer's music. The existing ornamentation is so Gallic that any supplementation of it in the repeats must be kept strictly in that style.

Johann Kuhnau (1660–1722), famous as Bach's predecessor as cantor of St. Thomas's Church in Leipzig, fascinates because of his bold ventures into areas which were only to be fully explored generations later. Many of the preludes to his partitas (suites in Bach's sense) are based on keyboard figurations taken up again in the time of Cramer and Clementi. In addition to the suites, Kuhnau also left what appear to be the first keyboard sonatas in the familiar multi-movement form. He appended one such sonata in 1692 to the partitas of the second part of his *Clavierübung*, a designation also used by Bach. Kuhnau is equally important in the development of programme music for the keyboard. His six *Biblical Sonatas* of 1700 recount in music such tales as the combat of David and Goliath. An acquaintance with Kuhnau's works will disclose some delightful pieces as well as some which seem rather naïve and perhaps second-rate when the inevitable comparisons are made.

The eleven suites of Georg Böhm (1661–1733), like those of Fischer, show considerable variety of structure. The second in *D* major opening with a French overture followed by a series of dances can still rouse listeners to great enthusiasm, especially with its powerful concluding chaconne. Certain others recall Froberger, notably the beautiful fifth suite in *E* flat major. Even if some fall below the highest standards, it is rewarding to know them—if only for the light they shed on the suites of Bach, who was strongly influenced by Böhm. Whether the chorale variations without pedal parts are real harpsichord music or not is difficult to say. But certainly the great Prelude, Fugue and Postlude in G minor is a masterpiece that should be played in a grand manner, for it is really a massive toccata.

We now return to France to survey the works of Chambonnières's successors. Louis Couperin (*c.* 1626–1661) might really have been considered at an earlier stage but his significance as a predecessor is even greater than his rank as a follower, most of all because he comes at the beginning of the great dynasty of musicians which included his nephew François, and only came to an end in the nineteenth century. His music remained largely unpublished until the twentieth century, though it ranks with the very greatest the seventeenth century produced, that is with the best of the virginalists, Sweelinck, Frescobaldi and Froberger. For sheer expressive power it is far more compelling still than Chambonnières at his best, although he founded the school and discovered the Couperin brothers, including Louis.

Except for a few organ pieces, some 'symphonies' for viols and other oddments, Louis Couperin's extant music is all for harpsichord. The order of the pieces in one modern edition seems arbitrary: after fourteen unmeasured preludes, discussed below, come dance pieces grouped in blocks by keys. Whether they were intended to be formally grouped into suites is not known; and the player must make his own groupings. While it is inconceivable that the movements of Bach's suites should be shuffled into an order different from the original one—and even more so with those of Mozart's or Beethoven's sonatas—with the pieces of Louis Couperin we have no choice but to put them into as logical and balanced an order as possible. No doubt the elder Couperin's death before the regular publication of harpsichord pieces in France (for Chambonnières did not bring his out until 1670) deprived him of an opportunity to put them into a definite sequence.

Part of the singular charm of older music is its demand that we should be actively creative and not merely dutifully accurate in its recreation. Unmeasured preludes, another form derived by the clavecinistes from their lutenist colleagues, are written in a strange notation showing only the pitch and overall phrasing of the notes, but not their duration. Actually, they are quite simple and very enjoyable to play once the knack has been mastered. The preludes consist of arpeggiated chords and scale passages, and are intended to define the tonality of the ensuing suite of dances. Not too many years ago, the last vestiges of this practice could still be encountered in the concert hall when pianists of the generation of Moriz Rosenthal and Josef Hofmann would often play a few arpeggios by way of a prelude to set the tonality, or in order to modulate between pieces in different keys.

After the preludes come the dance pieces, ranging from miniatures like *La Pastourelle* (no. 52) and *La Piémontoise* (no. 6) to pieces of such monumental grandeur as the mighty Pavan in *F* sharp minor (no. 100), the *Tombeau de M. de Blancrocher* (no. 84), the great chaconnes—notably those in *D* minor (nos. 54 and 63) and the one in *G* minor dated 1658 (no. 99)—and their close relations the Passacaglias, such as the *C* major one (no. 26). Just how closely the two are related is shown by the piece entitled *Chaconne ou Passacaille* in *G* minor (no. 96). Louis Couperin may be credited with the invention of the *pièce croisée*, that is, music to be played with one hand on each manual of a two-keyboard instrument; see, for example, the *C* major courante (no. 24). Certainly no earlier use of this device is known although the 'expressive double' harpsichord (as opposed to the 'transposing double' of the Ruckers family) may, in fact, prove to have existed even earlier than the time of Louis Couperin. (The numbers are from the Heugel edition.)

The works of Nicolas Lebègue (1630–1702) seem pallid against those of Louis Couperin. They consist of eleven suites published in 1675 and 1687. The outward form follows that established by Chambonnières; but in the first volume we also find the unmeasured prelude. A kind of precious over-refinement seems to flatten down the music. We search in vain for the grinding dissonances and richness of rhythmical variety of Louis Couperin, the very qualities which may have kept his music from gaining contemporary acceptance.

Jean-Henri d'Anglebert (1630–1691) writes in thicker instrumental textures than were regularly used by any other contemporary harpsichord composer. The sheer bulk of sound that this engenders may often seem to imply a musical value which is not actually present. In d'Anglebert's works, we find once again a seemingly endless set of variations on *Les Folies d'Espagne*, the *folia* ground bass used by so many others down to the time of Liszt's *Spanish Rhapsody*. Possibly in memorial tribute to Lully, d'Anglebert pioneered the operatic transcription—anticipating Liszt once more—by offering some *ouvertures et air célèbres* of the late composer in versions for harpsichord. But it is another elegy on the death of Chambonnières that assures d'Anglebert a place in the repertoire as well as in the history books. His *Tombeau* in memory of his teacher is a most deeply felt and moving tribute. His slow gavottes in minor keys, like the one entitled *Où êtes-vous allé*, are also strangely intense pieces.

THE EIGHTEENTH CENTURY

The active repertoire of the harpsichord today consists largely of works dating from the first half of the eighteenth century. Much of this music has never disappeared entirely from the concert hall, surviving even during the total dominance of the pianoforte during the nineteenth and early twentieth centuries. The keyboard works of the five greatest eighteenth-century composer-virtuosi make up a world of their own.

For sheer quantity Domenico Scarlatti takes the palm. We still possess some five hundred and fifty-five of his sonatas. Modern scholarship attributes fewer works to J. S. Bach than were included in the great nineteenth-century complete edition of the Bach Gesellschaft. Nevertheless the two volumes of the *Forty-Eight*, the harpsichord music in the *Clavierübung*, the fifteen or so additional suites, the seven toccatas, and the fantasies, preludes, fugues and miscellaneous pieces can fill many programmes. François Couperin's four books of *Pièces de Clavecin* contain twenty-seven 'ordres' with two hundred and twenty-nine individual pieces, some consisting of several movements. In comparison Rameau was far less generous, leaving us a mere forty-eight pieces for harpsichord, though what fine ones they are! Handel's works for harpsichord comprise some seventeen suites, six grand fugues and a large group of single pieces, including the great chaconnes. By a rough reckoning these five masters alone have bequeathed us over a thousand works for our instrument. When we reflect on the rest of their enormous output, particularly in the cases of Handel, Rameau and Bach, we stand amazed at the miracle of sheer fecundity which left them time and energy to compose so much harpsichord music, too.

Except for Bach, where the clavichord and perhaps the chamber organ, too, can claim a share, all this music is clearly conceived for harpsichord and for no other instrument. This is somewhat surprising, for the pianoforte had appeared on the scene as early as the first quarter of the century, and by the last quarter had practically eclipsed the harpsichord. This was certainly true of the harpsichord as a solo instrument, except possibly in France. Moreover, the suite as a form was in decline and on the point of succumbing to the sonata which became the dominant form of multi-movement piece for solo keyboard. While many lesser composers of the early eighteenth century did produce such multi-movement sonatas, for harpsichord as well as for clavichord and pianoforte, the illustrious 'five' did not.

A further astonishing fact is that three of these composers—Bach, Handel and Scarlatti—were all born in 1685. Rameau was born in 1683, fifteen years later than François Couperin, but his first publication of harpsichord music in 1706 was seven years in advance of Couperin's *Premier Livre de Pièces de Clavecin*. However, their respective periods of activity in the production of keyboard music varied. While Bach continued to write for the instrument throughout his life, Scarlatti is believed to have produced the bulk of his sonatas relatively late in life.

Let us begin with François Couperin (1668–1733), the senior member of the group. A nephew of Louis Couperin, he succeeded to the post of organist at the Church of Saint Gervais in Paris while still a boy and was named organist of the Chapel Royal in 1693. His whole life centred on Paris and the court of Versailles, where he taught the harpsichord to the royal princes and princesses, composed chamber and church music for the court, and found fame and even friendship among the great personages there.

Couperin's harpsichord method, *L'Art de Toucher le Clavecin*, is still of exceptional interest to the modern player. Of the great harpsichordists, only he and Rameau committed any thoughts on keyboard techniques to paper. The charming little allemande and eight preludes composed for this 'method' are very rewarding pieces to play. The preludes, Couperin indicates, can serve as such for 'ordres' in their respective tonalities.

The method appeared in 1716, just before Couperin put out his second book of pieces, dated 1717. Adopting his own procedure in the method where he had included a section giving fingerings for his first book of pieces dated 1713, Couperin followed the 1716 printing of *L'Art de Toucher* with a second, containing an additional section with fingerings for pieces in the latest book. He then asked people who owned copies of the first issue kindly to return them so that he could replace them with gratis copies of the second printing. This courteous gesture must have been well received, for no copy of the first issue is known to exist.

The four books of pieces appeared in 1713, 1717, 1722 and 1730 respectively, but many of them must have been composed much earlier, particularly those in the first and fourth volumes. What stimulated Couperin to publish them we cannot know for certain. During a brief five-year span from 1702 to 1707, one major composer, Rameau, and many of the lesser clavecinistes (Clérambault, Dieupart, Mme. Jacquet de la Guerre, Marchand and LeRoux) had all issued collections. But Couperin's first book must have come upon the scene like a comet, for during the seventeen years between its publication and the appearance of his fourth in 1730, only six other collections of harpsichord pieces appeared in Paris, a mere quarter of the number of those published in the same period after 1730. Some reluctance of his contemporaries to compete with Couperin le Grand, as he was known, can fairly be inferred.

Couperin is far more explicit in his directions for performance than any other composer for harpsichord. He puts in every single ornament. He provides indications of mood and tempo as well as picturesque titles, some of which now seem quite obscure. He expresses in the preface to Book III his desire that nothing should be added or omitted. Such a requirement of literal compliance with the printed page is accepted as a matter of course in our own time but was rare, if not virtually unknown, in the eighteenth century.

Without suggesting that it is simple to play Couperin well or that everything on the printed page is plain to the naked eye, one can state unequivocally that no filling-up is required of the player. In view of the composer's express command to the contrary, it would be highly presumptuous to vary the repeats of sections of a piece in the way that was generally expected by other composers. Yet Couperin grew up in the tradition of 'doubles' and even gives us a few of them in his earlier pieces. Possibly his strictures against adding or subtracting from the written notes were intended for the indifferent amateur performers of the day, those who could afford to pay up to 18 *livres* a volume for his printed music. The professional virtuoso performer of music composed by others did not yet exist. In the last analysis, good taste, *le bon goût*, which he himself designated as the court of final appeal in all matters musical, must be one's guide. To begin with, it is as well to approach his music in a conservative and literal spirit while still observing all the contemporary French performance conventions, especially unequal notes and overdotting.

The twenty-seven 'ordres' are anything but uniform in cut. They scarcely conform to the classic suite pattern. Some even contain suites within suites. Whether they should in every case be played as complete entities is therefore doubtful. The pieces from the shorter ordres, especially those which progress towards an obvious climax (e.g. no. 8 in *B* minor, and no. 24 in *A* major and minor, made up of ten and eight pieces, respectively) might suffer by performance out of context. An ordre like no. 2 in *D* minor with twenty-three pieces would obviously be indigestible played in its entirety. The outward form of most pieces is either the familiar binary structure or the rondeau, in which the initial theme is repeated throughout the piece after each contrasting 'couplet'. Somewhat puzzling are the pieces in several sections labelled 'First Part', 'Second Part' and so on. Should the first be repeated after the second has been played? In some cases no such repeat seems called for (e.g. 24th Ordre, *Les jeunes Seigneurs*). In others, it seems essential (e.g. 15th Ordre *Les Vergers fleuris*).

Couperin's sole registration instructions were provided for his *pièces croisées*, literally playable only on the uncoupled manuals of a double harpsichord with a single 8-foot register sounding on each. (For single manual instruments, Couperin directs that one part or the other should be transposed an octave). As to all the other pieces we can only surmise that they were composed with the standard French double instrument in mind, with 8- and 4-foot registers on the lower manual, a second 8-foot on the upper, and possibly a buff stop, all controlled by hand stops and a manual coupler. What a wealth of colour Couperin can draw from his instrument! Compare, for example, the contrasting sections of the great *Passacaille* in *B* minor (8th Ordre), the pieces worked out solely in a very low range like *La Bandoline* (5th Ordre) or the lute-like *Les Barricades Mystérieuses* (6th Ordre), those in a very high tessitura such as *Le Carillon de Cythère* (14th Ordre), and those which contrast high and low, like *La Convalescente* (26th Ordre).

Stylistically Couperin's pieces illustrate the transition from the grand baroque of Louis XIV's time to the rococo style of Louis XV's reign. French and Italian features reminiscent of the works of Lully and Corelli vie for dominance but the music remains essentially French. In their dimensions, too, the pieces vary greatly. If Couperin was formerly considered as a composer of little figurines in notes, that is probably because only his slightest pieces—those with the least tonal weight and musical substance—were the ones most readily transferable to the piano. Now that the harpsichord has returned, we can once more know Couperin in all his moods and styles, from the filigree to the monumental.

Although Jean-Philippe Rameau (1683-1764) has left us far fewer pieces for harpsichord than his elder compatriot Couperin, these have been, and still are, performed far more frequently. The reasons are not difficult to specify. Rameau paints his musical pictures in broad strokes, far broader than Couperin's. That is not to say, however, that where Couperin smiles, Rameau grimaces, or that what had been a sigh now becomes a torrent of tears. Rather it is that Rameau relies less on musical subtleties to make his points. The writing also has much more apparent virtuosity to offer the concert performer.

The catalogue of works is easily surveyed. The first book of pieces (1706) contains but a single suite in *A* minor, beginning with an unbarred prelude in the old style which gives way after a while to a $\frac{12}{8}$ Italianate gigue movement. Then come two allemandes, a courante, a gigue, two sarabandes played with a reprise of the first, as in a minuet and trio, and two more dances *en rondeau* concluding with a very simple and innocent minuet. All is on a relatively small scale.

The second book (1724) begins with an essay on the technique of playing the harpsichord. While differing from Couperin in detail, Rameau explains the basic touch in substantially similar terms. He also advocates completely 'modern' fingering, and provides a little *Menuet en Rondeau*, duly fingered, as a lesson. That lesson is quite elementary, and those who have need of such basic instruction will hardly be able to cope with the pieces which follow. First comes the great suite in *E* minor, one of the mainstays of the modern harpsichord repertoire, a perfectly balanced grouping of eight pieces: allemande, courante, two *gigues en rondeau*, *Le Rappel des Oiseaux*, two rigaudons with a *double* of the second, a charming *musette en rondeau*, the famous *tambourin*, and a rondeau *La Villageoise*. (Most performers, preferring to end the suite brilliantly, insert the last piece at an earlier point, either after the gigues or before the rigaudons.)

The second group of pieces in *D* major and minor can hardly be termed a suite, however. It comprises miniatures like the strangely ingenuous minuet *Le Lardon*, and two very extended works of considerable technical difficulty, *Les Niais de Sologne* and *Les Cyclopes*. Both require a wrist technique for playing arpeggio figures matched only among contemporary works by some of the sonatas of Scarlatti. It has often been said that *Les Cyclopes* was intended for two-manual performance. In fact, the literal notation, the musical requirements of the piece, and Rameau's preface, too, all seem to indicate the use of only the lower manual with a rather full registration.

Rameau's third book (*c.* 1728) begins with a suite grouping, this time in the major and minor modes of the key of *A*. Having opened with three classic dances, allemande, courante and sarabande, Rameau then gives us *Les Trois Mains*, a cross-hand *tour de force* as difficult as many of Scarlatti's. After a character piece and a sparkling rondeau, the group ends with the famous *Gavotte et Doubles*, a masterly set of six variations growing from a slow and rather sad gavotte tune in the d'Anglebert tradition to a conclusion of dazzling brilliance. The *batteries*, i.e. extended arpeggios requiring oscillating wrists and flying fingers, and the inexorable progress of the variations to their climax have made this piece a particular favourite of the public performer.

The eight pieces in G major and minor which follow include some of Rameau's choicest: *La Poule* with its famous imitation of the clucking of a hen (a musical tradition extending from the Middle Ages to the time of Walt Disney), *Les Sauvages* and *L'Enharmonique*, a bit of musical punning by Rameau the great harmonist and musical theoretician. While the markings of *doux* and *fort* in *La Poule* are clearly dynamic in intent, the *gracieusement* and *hardiment* of *L'Enharmonique* probably relate to mood and tempo rather than to dynamics as such.

Five pieces arranged for harpsichord solo from chamber works appeared in 1741, after which Rameau published no more harpsichord music. But we have, in addition, one of his improvisations, *La Dauphine*, composed at a royal wedding in 1747 and later set down on paper. It is a piece full of dramatic contrasts, very close in form to the classic sonata-allegro.

It is as ironic as it is regrettable that we today hear Rameau's harpsichord works, which he probably considered to be among his less important music, to the virtual exclusion of the rest of his considerable output. In the case of Scarlatti, whose best compositions are almost exclusively for the solo keyboard, or even in that of Couperin, where the pieces for harpsichord constitute such an important and representative portion of his oeuvre, it is immaterial how much the performer does or does not know of the other works. But with Rameau, just as with Bach and Handel, there is much to learn from the vast number of little-played sacred and secular cantatas, operas, ballets and pastorales. A few of Rameau's harpsichord pieces are actually used in or derived from stage works and an acquaintance with those other versions can contribute to a convincing performance on the harpsichord.

Four lesser clavecinistes contemporary with Couperin and Rameau deserve brief mention. Jean-François Dandrieu (1682–1738) published three books of pieces between 1718 and 1734. Like Couperin he combined the much appreciated Italian style with the French grand manner. A set of battle pieces, *Les Caractères de la Guerre* are less remarkable for their musical quality than for Dandrieu's instruction to use note-clusters in the bass to imitate cannon shots. *Le Concert des Oiseaux*, of lesser musical quality than the 'bird' pieces of Couperin and Rameau, is nonetheless quite charming. The grand baroque is exemplified in *La Lully*, a true French overture, perfect in form and style. Dandrieu's lyric side comes to the fore in pieces such as the lovely *La Gémissante* with its strange anticipation of Schubert's Gretchen singing at her spinning-wheel, and in *La Lyre d'Orphée* and *L'Affligée*. The few rare indications of registration are of particular interest.

François Dagincour (or d'Agincourt) (1684–1753) brought out a single book in 1733 with forty-three pieces grouped in four ordres. The influence of Couperin is apparent in the pieces about windmills, birds and giddy girls. The composer admits freely that his system of indicating articulation and ornaments is that of his illustrious predecessor. One piece, pointedly entitled *La Moderne* and mentioned especially by Dagincour in his preface, exhibits Italian traits closer to those of Rameau and the actual prototypes than to anything in Couperin's essays in the style of Corelli.

Louis Claude Daquin (1694–1772) has achieved a degree of immortality with one piece in his 1735 collection, *Le Coucou*, found in countless anthologies: a piquant rondo in *E* minor in unrelenting semiquavers. There are some charming light-weight pieces among the others, such as *La Mélodieuse* and *L'Hirondelle*.

Jacques Duphly (1715–1789), the last of the line, published his four books of forty-six pieces between 1744 and 1768. They include not only some delightful slighter works but also a number of serious extended pieces. *La Médée* is one of the best and indicates that

Duphly must have been well acquainted with Scarlatti's published works as well as with those of the earlier clavecinistes.

The more than five hundred sonatas of Domenico Scarlatti (1685–1757) fill eleven large volumes. We should not think, however, that he composed little else. In fact, the catalogue of his works includes listings of fifteen operas, numerous cantatas, oratorios, serenades, occasional pieces and liturgical works, all of which have disappeared from the repertoire. Indeed, they do not seem to have endured even in their own time. Many have vanished from the archives, so that it is truly through his sonatas alone that Scarlatti's immortality is assured. In 1738 when already fifty-three years of age he published the only authorised edition of his harpsichord pieces, a mere thirty sonatas (called, in this instance, *Essercizi*, i.e. 'lessons'). But many others circulated in manuscript, and groups of them were printed at various places during and after his lifetime. The bulk of the sonatas appear to have been composed after 1721, in the latter part of his life. In that year he left Italy for the court at Lisbon, and later moved on to Madrid when his patroness, a Portuguese princess, married the heir to the Spanish throne.

With a few exceptions, the form of the pieces conforms to a standard pattern that is basically binary. The first part works its way from the tonic to the dominant or the relative major in which it closes. The second part may begin with new material or with the development of previously heard motives, but in either case, it always ends with a concluding section that corresponds to that of the first part. Thus, no matter how far afield Scarlatti may roam at the beginning of the second part, he always returns to familiar ground well before the end of the piece.

No amount of description could do justice to the musical scope and variety of the sonatas. The rich variety of Scarlatti's Italian heritage and adopted Iberian culture is displayed in full. Their range, even within the limited form described above, seems infinite. It certainly goes far beyond the narrow bounds suggested by the older anthologies which tended to reprint the same few, mainly virtuoso pieces, drawn in large part from the *Essercizi* and other contemporary publications, and relieved by an occasional slow movement or other 'simpler' sonatas for the sake of the technically feeble.

3. Harpsichord by
Carlo Grimaldi, Messina, 1697
Dr. Ulrich Rück Collection of
Old Musical Instruments in
the Germanische
Nationalmuseum, Nuremberg

4. Spinet by John Harrison,
London, 1757
*Russell Collection of Early
Keyboard Instruments,
Edinburgh*

Ralph Kirkpatrick, the ranking authority, and a brilliant performer of Scarlatti's music in our time, has argued that all but the
first hundred or so sonatas (including the thirty *Essercizi*) in his
chronological catalogue were intended to be performed in pairs, or
occasionally in sets of three. Other performers and scholars, however, consider that the fact that the sonatas were so grouped by
tonalities in the principal sources (fair copies not in Scarlatti's hand)
does not necessarily impose an absolute duty to perform them in
pairs or threes. It sometimes happens that while one member of the
pair delights and enchants us, the other is less appealing. In such
instances it would seem too strict to insist that both members of
the pair should invariably be played.

In addition to providing the definitive study of Scarlatti and his
works, and a model edition of sixty sonatas, Kirkpatrick has by his
teaching and the example of his playing disposed of two noxious
'traditions': 'Blitz-tempos' and 'the automatic echo'. Because so
many nineteenth century athletes of the piano considered Scarlatti
only as a kind of instrumental trickster, every marking of allegro
was turned into a presto, while an indication of presto, in turn,
became a licence to play in 'Schumann tempo': 'as quickly as
possible—quicker—and still quicker', the famous indications in his
sonata Opus 22. The 'automatic echo' was again introduced by
pianists who, already somewhat deprived of expressive possibilities
by their choice of exaggeratedly fast tempi, had little recourse but
to vary the repetition of a two, four or eight bar passage by playing
it in a feathery pianissimo by way of relief from the hammered-out
forte of its first appearance. So ingrained have both these false
doctrines become that it will probably be many years yet before
we hear the last of them.

The evidence shows plainly that Scarlatti must for the most part
have composed his pieces for, and performed them on, single-
manual instruments, usually with one or two 8-foot stops. Such
double harpsichords as he might have had available probably did
not possess the necessary compass for the later sonatas, in particular,
which demand a full five octaves, *FF–f'''* and *GG–g'''*, respectively.
Thus the 'automatic echo' could not often have been in the composer's contemplation. Even the notorious cross-hand passages,

5

especially prevalent in the earlier sonatas, rarely require two manuals for performance and often do not permit their use for purely dynamic reasons.

Technically speaking, a number of the sonatas make demands which recall John Bull and look ahead to Franz Liszt and even Alkan. Scales, arpeggios, leaps, single and double trills, thirds, sixths and octaves all abound and require a complete virtuoso technique. Yet, to our surprise and delight, there are dozens and dozens of sonatas which ask only for modest technical equipment, though demanding great musical perception. Two of the loveliest sonatas are also amongst the easiest in terms of technical difficulty: *A* major, Kirkpatrick 322 (L. 483), and *D* minor, Kirkpatrick 32 (L. 423). Yet these were often played by Vladimir Horowitz, a rare connoisseur of Scarlatti amongst contemporary pianists, and by Wanda Landowska, neither of whom could be considered technically deficient.

Whether Scarlatti really had pupils and disciples outside the royal circle is a matter of controversy. Stylistic elements associated primarily with his works also occur in the keyboard music of his Iberian contemporaries and followers. The works of one Spanish composer, Padre Antonio Soler (1729–1783), and one minor Portuguese master, Carlos de Seixas (1704–1742), are well worth exploring. About a hundred or so sonatas by Soler have been published together with a single very extended fandango. Soler, for all his virtuoso tricks—he may well have studied for five years as a pupil of Scarlatti's learning them all—actually spent his life as organist and choirmaster at the Royal Monastery of the Escorial. He may seem to lack the brevity of true wit and run on a bit too long on occasion. But at his best Soler's sonatas offer very grateful writing for the harpsichord coupled with considerable intensity of feeling.

Seixas left us far fewer pieces, if the eighty published sonatas are a true guide, and he died at the age of twenty-eight. Had Scarlatti died so young, we might have had not a single sonata from him but only a handful of now forgotten larger works. Seixas keeps within relatively modest bounds, technically and musically, adding occasional delightful touches of Portuguese colour.

We know that George Frideric Handel (1685–1759) met Scarlatti, probably in Rome in 1709, and while their match at the harpsichord was generally considered to have resulted in a draw, the Saxon's superiority at the organ was clear to all. Handel was doubtless at the height of his powers as an improviser and executant at that time. In his later years he was occupied with the composition and production of his operas, oratorios, occasional pieces and all the other works in his enormous output. He then very rarely appeared at the keyboard in public except in connection with the performance of one of his larger works.

The first authorised publication of his harpsichord music took place in 1720 and was very likely timed to forestall a threatened pirated edition. But all the first eight suites then issued may well have been composed much earlier. We know that certain movements were written long before. For example, the highly decorated Air in the third suite in *D* minor also exists in its pristine, utterly simple form of an earlier day.

The publication of the second volume of suites and pieces followed in 1733, without the composer's permission. Handel authorised the publication of the six great fugues in 1735, but all the other works for solo keyboard that came out in one form or another during his lifetime were apparently published without his knowledge or consent.

The eight suites offer an astounding array of styles. Immediately we recognise in Handel one of the two great eclectic masters of his time, the other, of course, being J. S. Bach. The French dances, the Lully-type overture, the free prelude of the lutenists stand alongside the Corelli-type jig, the full *sonata da chiesa* form, and movements in concerto style. Associated with these we also find movements strongly influenced by the polyphonic tradition of the German organists, such as Zachau, Handel's teacher back in Halle, where Scheidt had presided at the organ two generations earlier. Only one of these suites, the second in *E* minor, contains the complete quartet of dances in the classic suite form. The synthesis of diverse styles, rather wider in scope than Couperin's *goûts réunis*, combined with the immediacy and complete accessibility of Handel's music, delights us today as much as it did his contemporary audience. The fact that the technical demands of the pieces are not excessive, although musically they require all we can give, has also contributed to their popularity ever since 1720. It would be an error to seek the subtlety of Couperin or the inner intensity of Bach in the works of Handel. Despite the domestic quality which pervades his solo and chamber music alike, these compositions are above all the work of a man of the world.

The second volume of suites and pieces published in 1733 comprises nine numbers. The first consists of a prelude followed by an aria (famous for its use by Brahms in his *Handel Variations*), and five variations, all in B flat major, followed by a minuet in G minor. This obviously incongruous arrangement must stem from the publisher, not the composer. The minuet is best played elsewhere, possibly in the G minor suite (no. 6 of the pieces in this volume), which has only three movements. The second portion of the collection is devoted to the Chaconne in G major with twenty-one variations, one of Handel's most substantial harpsichord pieces. This piece was first published in a pirated edition, for the last bars, at the end of the twenty-first variation, are notated in obviously sketched form. To play them as written would be comparable to ending a firework display by lighting a kitchen-match. Handel's harpsichord music, alone among that of the great 'five', often requires considerable supplementation through freely improvised additions, to supply both tonal reinforcement and ornamental decoration.

Next follow six suites of uneven quality. Some movements are among the best that came from Handel's pen, while others are of a sort that might have thrilled those who listened to his improvisations at the moment of creation, though they can drive a modern performer to distraction. The final piece in the set is a chaconne, again in G major, followed by sixty-two (!) variations. This may be a record, probably incomplete, of a Handelian improvisation. The eight-measure bass is a familiar formula, used by Purcell in one of his grounds and even by Bach in the theme of the *Goldberg Variations*. Opinions as to the performability of this Chaconne are divided, for it is clearly not a finished work. It neither builds up logically to a final climax, in the usual 'grand manner', nor does it fade away like the grin of the Cheshire cat. It would be a pity to leave it unplayed; we need not hesitate to change the order of the variations or even to make a selection from them in the interests of a more satisfying musical structure.

The six fugues of 1735 are superb examples of the form as Handel practised it. Although he left us no *Forty-Eight*, these half-dozen suffice to establish that he was as much a master of the fugal texture in keyboard music as in choral and orchestral movements. Yet these fugues are rarely performed, perhaps because they lack preludes. The G minor capriccio from the third collection would make an excellent prelude to the first fugue in that key; or one might also play it after the fugue, prefacing the pair with the *Preludio ed Allegro*, also in G minor and found in the same volume.

Other individual pieces, such as the Fantasia in C major and Lesson in A minor from the third collection, will be found most rewarding to play. The *Aylesford Pieces*, first published in 1928, offer a miscellany of seventy-six works ranging from very short and simple pieces to quite elaborate essays in larger forms. It is a collection heartily recommended to all Handelians. The somewhat random and sketchy qualities of the anthology do not detract from its musical worth. But we should not rest content with merely playing the printed notes. Considerable creative effort by the performer is called for as well.

From Raymond Russell's exhaustive treatment of the subject, we know that the claim of various instruments to have been 'Handel's harpsichord' are rather dubious. In his early days in Germany, he no doubt played all types of instrument, single and double, possibly even some of the very large Hamburg harpsichords during his stay in that city. In Italy, of course, there were very few double harpsichords, but the full range of instruments available in England included, in Handel's latter years, the famous large English two-manual instruments of Shudi and Kirckman.

In registration Handel seems to allow us the widest latitude of any of the great 'Five'. We should, however, not lose sight of the fact that, except in variations, where stops could be manipulated more frequently, Handel must have played his longer movements, fugues and suite dances without the frequent registration changes often heard today; indeed he could often have made none at all. There is no evidence that Handel ever had anything but hand stops available to him and we should be guided accordingly. As in so much of the best keyboard music, the registration is written into the work itself. The dynamics result from the alternate thickening and thinning of the texture of the music. Constant changes of registration are thus unnecessary. Even a long chaconne can often be effectively performed on two or at most three levels of tone.

Georg Philipp Telemann (1681–1767) was one of Handel's life-long friends. His career took him from his native Magdeburg round much of Northern Germany—eventually to Hamburg. There he served as cantor and music director of the five principal churches until his death, when he was succeeded by his godson, Carl Philipp Emanuel Bach, the second son of Johann Sebastian. While his total output of music was prodigious, Telemann's known keyboard works are relatively few. Possibly more will come to light as the collected edition of his music progresses.

The *Three Dozen Fantasies* are really somewhat more in the style of operatic overtures, both French overtures and Italian sinfonias, while the *Six Overtures* are actually suites, not in the 'classic' form to be sure, but groups of pieces—mainly dances—prefaced by French overtures. With access to virtually the entire range of keyboard music of all periods and schools, we need not linger too long over Telemann. A few of the dances are quite charming. The short fugues are fluent in style but quite impersonal. The larger works seem pale next to those of the illustrious 'Five'.

Finally we come to the greatest synthesiser of all, Johann Sebastian Bach (1685–1750). Our survey must of necessity be brief because there are so many categories of works and individual pieces to mention. In the case of Bach there is no need to reassure the reader about the quality of the music. Even the least of his works stand very high by the best that lesser figures of the time produced.

The *Forty-Eight*, the preludes and fugues known collectively as the *Well-Tempered Clavier* consist of two volumes, assembled but not necessarily composed in 1722 (BWV 846–869) and 1744 (BWV 870–893) respectively. Each contains twenty-four preludes and fugues in each of the major and minor keys. Like so much of Bach's music, these were composed with a didactic purpose in mind. The title page of the autograph of Part I of the *Forty-Eight* states that the twenty-four preludes and fugues are offered 'for the benefit and use of musical young people who are eager to learn and of those, too, who are already skilled in this subject'.

There is no need to catalogue the preludes and fugues, for many volumes of commentaries and analyses are available. It is generally considered that the *Forty-Eight*, and the second volume in particular, represent a summation of Bach's art which, in turn, can be characterised as the grand synthesis of styles and forms in the mid-eighteenth century. The titles 'prelude' and 'fugue' suggest abstract, colourless, even crabbed writing, at least to the uninitiated. In the case of the *Forty-Eight* nothing could be further from the truth. Fugues in the form of a passepied or a gigue hardly come under the heading of dry, scholarly, recondite music. Even those written in the old ricercar style are highly charged, building up section by section to powerful climaxes. Preludes in the guise of overtures, toccatas— and even of arias and choruses like those of the cantatas and passions —are found alongside smaller and simpler movements. Bach seems never to repeat himself in all the ninety-six pieces making up the two volumes.

From the point of view of keyboard technique, these eight dozen pieces include some that demand great virtuosity while others are within the grasp of almost every player. Where virtuosity is required, it is very different from that required by Rameau or Scarlatti; the emphasis is rarely placed on sheer velocity or mere digital skill in executing awkward figurations. But the harpsichordist who can lucidly delineate every line of the fugues of the *Forty-Eight* can fairly claim to have attained mastery of his instrument.

As an introduction to polyphonic keyboard performance, and as teaching material for his own sons, Bach composed the fifteen two-part inventions (BWV 772-786) and the fifteen three-part inventions or sinfonias (BWV 787-801). They, together with some short preludes and fugues, some of which were later included in Book I of the *Forty-Eight*, first appear in their original form in the *Clavier-büchlein für Wilhelm Friedemann Bach*. It was later that they were given the definitive form in which they are nowadays invariably studied and performed. If any keyboard music deserves to be considered as indispensable, especially to harpsichordists, it is these thirty inventions. Do not be put off by their professed didactic purpose. The inventions offer a degree of musical interest not to be found in any other self-professed 'teaching pieces' before Bartók's *Mikrokosmos*, also written for the composer's son.

We should ponder Bach's inscription on the title page of the autographs of the final version of the inventions. Freely translated from the quaint German, it describes the contents as 'straightforward instruction whereby amateurs of the keyboard, and especially those eager to learn, are clearly shown not only (1) to learn to play distinctly in two parts, but also after progress (2) to deal properly and well with three independent parts; furthermore, at the same time not only to invent good musical ideas but also to develop them well, and most of all to attain a cantabile style in playing, as well as to acquire a firm grounding in composition'. The singing style of performance is not only Bach's main concern as a pedagogue but holds the key to the musical delights of the inventions as well.

The six suites known as the *French Suites* (BWV 812-817) also formed part of the domestic musical repertoire of the Bach family. Five of them appear in the 1722 *Clavierbüchlein* of Anna Magdalena, Bach's second wife. All six are complete classic suites with allemande, courante, sarabande and gigue movements, supplemented by other dances interpolated after the sarabande. They have no preludes. While no doubt strongly influenced by French works in the same form, these suites could hardly be mistaken for anything other than music by Bach. Not all the dances are actually French; several of the courantes are really in the Italian form of the dance, the 'corrente' based on a running figure and without the ambiguous interplay of duple and triple rhythms of the French variety. Two similar short suites in *A* minor and *E* flat major (BWV 818-819) are delightful to play, too. Why they are not performed more often is really quite beyond explanation.

The six so-called *English Suites* (BWV 806-811) are in some ways far more Gallic in style and feeling than their simpler and briefer

'French' brethren. Not only are the dances longer, more elaborately worked out and much closer to the real French tradition, but each is prefaced by an extensive prelude as well. Yet, except for the one to the first suite in *A* major, these preludes are in Italian concerto-grosso style. The 'doubles' and alternate ornamented versions which Bach provided for two of the sarabandes are perfect models for those who wish to vary reprises in the manner of the period.

The six partitas (BWV 825-830) another series of suites in the expanded classical form, are also prefaced by introductory movements, each with a different title and form: Praeludium, Sinfonia, Fantasia, Ouverture, Praeludium and Toccata. They were issued by Bach between 1726 and 1730 as part of his Opus 1, so designated because it was his first publication of his own music. They form the first part of the *Clavierübung* (literally 'keyboard exercises'), a title previously used by Kuhnau, Bach's predecessor at his Leipzig church, recalling Scarlatti's title of *Essercizi* for his publication of thirty sonatas. In publishing these partitas, Bach must have recognised that they crown his essays in the suite form and represent a synthesis of all elements and national styles, not merely French but Italian and German as well.

In the *Italian Concerto* (BWV 971) and *French Overture* (BWV 831) published a few years later as the second part of the *Clavierübung*, Bach presents the perfect keyboard realisations of two of the prevailing orchestral forms, the Italian concerto grosso and the French orchestral suite, beginning with an overture in the manner of Lully. The *Concerto* has long been a staple of the piano repertoire, though less so in recent years since more frequent performances on the harpsichord have shown that the piece succeeds rather better on the original instrument for which it was expressly written. However, the *French Overture* did not take so kindly to translation to the later instrument and was thus rarely performed before the revival of the harpsichord. It is a work that exploits all the resources of the two-manual instrument in the fullest sense, even more amply than the *Concerto*.

The four duets (BWV 802-805) are comparatively little-known, probably because they form part of the third instalment of the *Clavierübung*—which also includes eighteen chorale preludes and the

mighty *Prelude and Fugue in E flat* ('St Anne's') for organ. Musico-
logists have adduced evidence to show that the duets were intended
as liturgical music but there is no denying their suitability for the
harpsichord. These giant two-part inventions merit the closest
study. As keyboard pieces they show the manifold possibilities,
both harmonic and contrapuntal, of writing in this most restrictive
of polyphonic textures. On the musical level they are to be ranked
amongst Bach's most polished and most moving pieces, a perfect
union of his art and his craft.

The *Aria with Thirty Variations* (BWV 988), known popularly
as the *Goldberg Variations* because of the Bach pupil of that name for
whom they were supposedly commissioned, make up the fourth
and final section of the *Clavierübung*. Even for the harpsichordist
who cannot hope to perform them, either because of his own
limitations or those of his instrument—the work demands a full-
size double harpsichord—there is infinite beauty and wisdom to be
derived from their study. Not only the prodigious technical demands
of the work—probably the most exacting of any written for the
harpsichord—but even more its musical requirements will always
reserve it for the happy few capable of presenting it as a unified and
integral structure. In a composition which requires over an hour for
complete performance, observing all repeats, that is no mean task.

The aria on which the variations are based can, on the other hand,
be approached by a player of modest capacities who possesses only
a small harpsichord. It was originally part of the Bach family's
domestic musical repertoire, appearing in the later *Clavierbüchlein*
of Anna Magdalena, dated 1725, some seventeen years before the
variations appeared in print. This beguiling aria is really a sarabande
in the French manner, not unlike those in the G major French suite
and the partita in the same key. It is a model of Bach's art of musical
decoration, well worth learning as a study in the playing of
ornaments.

The seven toccatas (BWV 910-916) are basically similar in form,
although they differ in fine points of construction. They all begin in
the traditional manner with a scale or passage in a single part which
grows into a kind of improvisatory prelude. All conclude with at
least one full-blown fugue. What happens in between these outer

limits varies; usually a slower canzona or other contrapuntal section followed by an arioso is interpolated. In the case of the G major toccata (BWV 916), Bach cloaks the form in concerto grosso trappings. In the C minor toccata (BWV 911) he adds a second double fugue of most powerful effect. As befits the genre, these are instrumentally conceived pieces, intended to display the performer's prowess and the qualities of his instrument. In Bach's case these considerations do not detract in any way from the musical interest of the pieces, and no concessions to mere outward virtuosity are involved. The toccatas are rewarding to study and unfailingly successful in performance.

The *Chromatic Fantasy and Fugue* (BWV 903) is somewhat related to the toccata form but the fantasy section is considerably less tightly structured. It closes with a long recitative section, a single, highly melismatic vocal line alternating with heavy chords. Just because the fantasy is so imaginative and free it is well to point up the contrast by playing the fugue in a simple and classical manner up to the coda, where the fantasy spirit takes over for the last few bars, rounding off and unifying the entire work. While the fantasy can survive almost any degree of registration pedal-pushing, it can be very excitingly and movingly performed without introducing new tone colourings and dynamic levels in every phrase. The freedom that is called for is far better expounded through subtleties of touch, tempo and rhythm.

The sixteen concerti (BWV 972-987) arranged from orchestral works by Vivaldi, Marcello, Telemann and others of Bach's contemporaries are rather a mixed lot of pieces. A few of them have proved viable concert numbers, notably the first in D major based on Vivaldi's op. 3 no. 7, and the third in D minor, based on an oboe concerto of Alessandro Marcello's, originally in C minor. The latter is particularly famous for its lovely slow movement which Bach ornamented with particular grace and elegance. But the quality of the concertos is so uneven that doubts have been expressed concerning the authenticity of some of them.

The *Fantasy and Fugue in A minor* (BWV 904) is an undeservedly neglected major masterpiece, a work of the finest quality that should be taken up by every harpsichordist capable of playing it. The

tightly-knit fantasy is in the style of some of Frescobaldi's movements, a piece of five-part contrapuntal writing unequalled in
Bach's keyboard works except for the six-part ricercar in the
Musical Offering and certain fugues in the old, strict style among
the *Forty-Eight*. The fantasy is followed by a double fugue on an
equally sublime plane.

   The *Fantasy in C minor* (BWV 906), another of the pieces playable
only on a double harpsichord, is a brilliant and unique example of
Bach's keyboard style. It has often been compared to the sonatas
of Domenico Scarlatti because of its form—very close to that of the
Neapolitan master—and the use of hand crossings which in this
case plainly require two keyboards. The autograph of the fantasy
is followed by the torso of an extraordinarily daring chromatic
fugue which, regrettably, breaks off abruptly.

   The *Capriccio on the Departure of a Beloved Brother* (BWV 992) is
one of Bach's early works, recalling the style of Kuhnau. It dates
from 1704, when Bach was only nineteen, and was written when
Johann Jakob Bach left home to enter the service of Charles XII
of Sweden. The little set of pieces is quite frankly programmatic,
with descriptions in music of the lamentations of the family and
friends, the postillion's horn call—finally transformed into the
kernel of the subject of the concluding fugue—and similar naïve
but charming domestic scenes attendant on the brother's departure.
Apart from a few crudities—such as some exposed parallel fifths in
the fourth section—this sincere and utterly ingenuous piece can
delight both performer and listener.

   The solo keyboard music of Germany after Bach's time tended
largely to move in directions less suited to the harpsichord than to
its successors, the early fortepiano and the large Northern European
clavichords of the period. While the harpsichord continued for
twenty years or more after Johann Sebastian's death to dominate
ensemble music, the spirit of solo keyboard music had undergone
fundamental change. The solo pieces of Bach's sons and pupils,
while they can be managed up to a point on modern instruments
with pedal registration, really belong to the new era which had
dawned with the invention of the pianoforte.

   Thus, in the truest sense, the classic solo harpsichord repertoire comes to an end with the demise of the great 'five' of the eighteenth century. Many of their finest works were, in fact, written after the time when the newer keyboard instruments and changing aesthetic currents of the period had already sealed the fate of the older instrument.

THE TWENTIETH CENTURY

From the middle of the eighteenth century to the last years of the nineteenth the harpsichord slumbered. Occasional use in 'historical' concerts of 'antient musick' did not stimulate composers to write new music for the instrument. They could hardly have been expected to do so, since the aesthetic of the romantic era was utterly contrary in spirit to that of the harpsichord. After all, the music which succeeds best on the harpsichord is music of line rather than mass, music that exploits the instrument's capacity for rhythmical precision and sinewy articulation, rather than exposing its inability to produce lush, velvety sonorities and dynamic inflections ranging from the most delicate nuances to the starkest of contrasts.

The anti-romantic aesthetic trend in music which emerged in the early twentieth century coincided with the revival of the harpsichord. Busoni, a leader in the revolt against romanticism, was probably the first composer of our time to write for harpsichord—in his opera *Die Brautwahl*, composed around 1912. He later produced a sonatina supposedly composed for harpsichord but actually unperformable on it and clearly written for piano. He then abandoned the plucked stringed keyboard.

Delius was probably the next to attach the words 'for harpsichord' to a piece of music—his *Dance* of 1919 commissioned by Violet Gordon-Woodhouse. Whatever the merits of the music, it is utterly unsuited to the harpsichord. It obviously requires a piano, especially for the sake of the damper pedal which the music clearly demands.

Just as in the last glow of the harpsichord's classic period and even afterwards, as late as 1802, when Beethoven's sonatas opus 31 were published as *pour clavecin ou pianoforte*, much of what has been brought forth recently as 'for harpsichord or piano' is actually idiomatic only for the latter instrument. It is a rare composer who, like Henze in his *Lucy Escott Variations* (1963), troubles to write a separate version of a piece for each.

The total separation of the personalities of composer and performer that characterises our time, with only rare exceptions such as Busoni and Rachmaninoff among pianists, and Daniel Pinkham among harpsichordists, presents a striking contrast to the age of Couperin and Scarlatti. Gone are the royal, noble or bourgeois pupils and patrons who provided composer-virtuosi-instructors with an opportunity to create, perform and teach works of music. Except for the rare commission from foundations and festivals, most contemporary music for harpsichord has been created at the behest of performers whose musical interest has encompassed the world of the present as well as of the past.

In a real sense, twentieth-century music for harpsichord can be said to begin with Manuel de Falla. Like Busoni, Falla first used the instrument in a work for the musical theatre but then went on to write a concerto, really a sextet, for Wanda Landowska which was first performed in 1926. Despite almost insuperable difficulties of dynamic balance, the concerto stands as a landmark and deserves more frequent performance.

It would be easy to adopt a condescending attitude towards pioneering efforts at composing for the harpsichord, just as some are supercilious about certain early recorded performances of older music by the generation of Dolmetsch and Landowska. But in an age still so dominated by the pianoforte, the ubiquitous maid-of-all-work of music, it has been particularly difficult for composers to free themselves from the instrumental technique and aesthetics of the keyboard at which so many of them do their daily work. Contemporary writing for harpsichord has generally been more successful in the chamber ensemble than in either the solo domain or that of the concerto. No modern harpsichord solo has yet established itself in the repertoire. Few indeed are the contemporary pieces using the harpsichord that have become familiar to concert audiences, but that, alas, is true of so much of the music of our time. It is ironic indeed that Elliott Carter's *Double Concerto* of 1961 which many connoisseurs have pronounced a masterpiece—Stravinsky has even said so in print—attempts the impossible by pitting the harpsichord against the modern pianoforte. Frank Martin's *Petite Symphonie Concertante* of 1945 had anticipated Carter in a sense by using harpsichord, piano and harp as solo instruments against a double string orchestra. Much contemporary harpsichord music is beyond the capacities of any but the most accomplished performers. Still, there are pieces which demand only modest technical equipment, though at the same time considerable musical intelligence and feeling. (See, for instance, the volume of *Neue Cembalomusik*, Bärenreiter Edition, no. 3804.) Most of the more elaborate works have been written with correspondingly complex instruments in mind. But composers are coming to recognise that it is unwise to specify particular types of harpsichord or registration. The harpsichord has only a few stops and combinations available. Composers should understand that the harpsichord's dynamic range can best be exploited by thinking primarily in terms of textures and tessitura rather than of registration. Adding registers one by one produces a crescendo only in a very limited sense. The addition of an octave stop has nothing to do with the sound of octaves played as such.

An article by Michael Steinberg of 1963 in *Perspectives of New Music* listed more than one hundred and fifty composers who had contributed to the modern repertoire for harpsichord. By now the number may well have doubled. From the least pretentious two-part little solo for domestic music-making to such monster ensemble works as John Cage's *HPSCHD* (1968), calling for seven amplified harpsichords used in a massive electronic ensemble, contemporary composers have produced a broad range of pieces for the instrument. There is much stimulus and enjoyment to be derived from coming to know this more recent music for harpsichord. It adds spice and excitement to our repertoire of pieces to introduce contemporary rhythms and sonorities.

IV

MASTERING THE BASIC TOUCH

Although the reader is presumed to have some notions of keyboard technique, most likely as applied at the pianoforte, it seems advisable nonetheless to begin with fundamentals, viewing technique for the moment in its limited sense as the mechanics of keyboard playing.

All pianofortes of modern construction are basically so similar, at least in their respective grand and upright forms, that one can generalise rather freely about them. But harpsichords, modern and antique alike, offer bewildering variations in such fundamental features as weight and depth of touch, length and width of keys, degree of inertia, type of plectrum material, string tension and key covering material. This fact limits the degree to which one can generalise about the technique of playing the harpsichord.

First of all make sure that you are sitting properly at the instrument. The seat may have a back or not, but it must in any case be firm and not softly upholstered. You should have the feeling of being firmly in the saddle, comfortably and solidly supported. Soft cushions must be avoided. The seat should be about ten inches below the level of the keys (lower manual), and some ten inches in front of them should be available for the player to move hands and arms freely to the ends of the keyboard. In the case of a corpulent person a tactical retreat of several inches may be necessary. Even for those who are slender some experimentation is called for, taking due account of the relative length of the spinal column and arms. The optimum position is one which is not only initially comfortable and solid, but also permits and fosters the most efficient movement of the entire playing mechanism, in effect the whole torso. At a two-manual instrument you should take the higher level of the upper keyboard into account and choose a position that will not hamper you in moving to and from the second manual and playing upon it.

The line from the elbow along the forearm to the knuckles of the hand should be almost straight, possibly with a slight downward inclination. To develop a sense of a proper hand position, concentrate at first on the contact of the thumb and little finger with the keys. The other three inner fingers will naturally fall into place over their keys. The best and most natural position is obtained by placing the fingers easily over the keys as indicated in the example.

Ex. 2

Fix the sensation of this normal position in your mind. It will only have to be modified substantially when playing at the extreme bass or treble end of the keyboard. To the extent practicable, the fingertips should be kept relatively close to the forward edge of the keys.

The basic touch of the harpsichord is easy to acquire but the adaptability of students varies. Just as there are drivers who can change from one car to another with little or no difficulty, there are keyboard players who can easily move from their normal instrument to another and adapt to it almost instantly. For others it is more difficult. If what you feel when playing and what you hear are both satisfying and not in any way painful, the chances are that the adaptation has been successful. If not, then it is best to stop immediately, and attempt to diagnose then correct the fault. Playing the harpsichord requires far less force than playing the pianoforte. Focus on the ease of playing. Avoid anything that will inhibit or cramp your freedom of movement. Remain gently poised without

6

strain from your neck muscles and shoulders down to your finger tips.

The essential rule of the basic harpsichord touch is that the entire playing force is provided in principle by the fingers alone, with the rest of the playing mechanism—forearm, upper arm, shoulder and trunk—employed solely to position the hand over the keys and to help it move from one position to another. To cite one homely parallel, the same use of the arm from shoulder to wrist is made in the process of ironing clothes. The stroke of the finger is made from the knuckle joint which connects the finger to the hand (the metacarpo-phalangeal joint). No application of weight to the keys is involved; indeed, that will not only detract from the mechanical efficiency of the entire process, but will also have a most deleterious effect on the tone produced. There will be a thump at the bottom of the key's descent if you drop onto the key with any weight.

You will know at once whether this basic rule of playing with the fingers alone is being observed for you will feel a sense of having worked in the knuckles that lie at the roots of the fingers. This is not at all a painful sensation but only an awareness of heightened muscle tone, the result of having alternately tensed and relaxed muscles in a controlled and conscious manner.

A second basic rule which virtually assures observance of the first one is: keep your fingers close to the keys. By doing so and maintaining at the same time a naturally curved hand position, proper touch is more or less assured. The basic naturally curved position of the hand is what we see when the arms are hanging down at our sides, possibly with the slightest additional grasping flexion.

But a cautionary word is needed here. Some of the greatest exponents of the harpsichord in recent times—great, too, in terms of public acceptance of their artistry—have used hand positions which involve an exaggerated measure of finger curving. Their fingers, flexed to the maximum, have often appeared to have risen almost to the perpendicular from sunken knuckles and then to have attacked the keys with a lightning down-stroke that, for all its precision, has not achieved a noiseless touch. The emphasis may have seemed to be placed far more on 'attack' than on 'touch'.

Individual hands certainly differ greatly. One should recognise this fact as well as respect the renown of certain players who have used this seemingly unnatural, even bizarre hand position, resembling in extreme cases the contractures of rheumatoid arthritis. But great harm can be done by trying to imitate them, certainly at the start.

It is better, rather, to work forward from a naturally arched hand, keeping the finger tips as close to the keys as possible, moving the fingers from the first knuckle joint, and limiting the participation of arm from shoulder to wrist to a weightless, positioning, balancing rôle. We must feel that we are really playing on the strings rather than on the keys. Every aspect of touch should relate to linking the finger, indeed the whole body of the player, to the key mechanism so intimately as to foster that feeling.

In time, when these principles have been assimilated and are being consistently applied, a certain degree of added tension in the fingers and hand, even a higher finger stroke, can be tolerated. To some degree it may prove helpful in achieving precision. But for the beginner this will more often lead to strain, muscle cramps and utter despair.

Even more to be avoided, obviously, is any raising of the arm so as to cause the hand to pounce upon the keyboard like the claw of a bird of prey. Not only will that result in mechanical inefficiency —the up and down motions of the arm take time—but also in an ugly, noisy tone and a nasty knocking sound at the end of the stroke. Dive-bombing the keyboard generally does not work.

It is best to begin on a single register, as François Couperin pointed out two hundred and fifty years ago in his harpsichord method. This should be an 8-foot stop, the lower manual one on a double harpsichord, voiced as softly as possible. It is far easier to develop a proper legato touch, the fundamental harpsichord touch, when the resistance of the plectrum to the string is minimal. Use the gentlest plucking action and sound that the instrument affords.

Begin by playing a few conventional five-finger patterns slowly, following the basic rules given above, and keeping the fingers close to the front of the keys.

Ex. 3

Play with only one hand at a time. Transpose patterns (a), (b) and (c) into various keys, especially E flat major in the left hand and F sharp minor in the right hand.

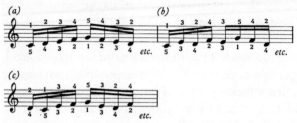

Immediately you will note the relatively light weight and feel of the action. The gentlest of pressures will depress the key to the point where the plectrum impinges on the string. Then, a slight additional pressure will cause it to pluck and pass on to the point where the jack or the key, respectively, reaches the end of its motion. The fingers should be raised slightly, less than an inch above the surface of the key, then brought quickly down to that surface and beyond to the point where the plectrum is actuated.

Pay close attention to the timing of the release as well as to that of the attack of each note. The necessary duration of the note is assured by gentle pressure of the finger on the key, acting solely by its own controlled muscular force and without any resting on the key with application of weight. The release involves merely the removal of that slight pressure and the return of the finger to the normal hand position level prior to its being raised before its next descent.

Listen carefully to the release of a single note. Try to discern how the damping process operates and how the various elements of the sound, fundamentals and partials, are extinguished. (Modern harpsichords usually damp rather more abruptly and completely than antique instruments, by the way.) You will note that extremely short staccatos, such as can be produced with ease on the pianoforte with good musical effect, do not succeed on the harpsichord which, in this sense, rather resembles bowed string instruments. A certain minimum duration of sound is needed for the production of the proper tone quality.

After learning how a single sound is produced, the next step is to learn to connect two notes. One remark of Mme. Landowska's has been cited in this context: 'My staccato is always legato.' Even where there is a silence between two notes, you must nevertheless sense the connection, the ligation which binds them nonetheless. This sense of the linking of each two consecutive notes must first be developed from a super-legato before it can be extended mentally and physically to the connexion of tones actually separated by an interval of silence.

The harpsichord is supposed to be incapable of any dynamic nuance. By careful timing of attacks and releases of successive notes, illusions of the acoustically impossible can be produced. For example, let us try to produce a 'sighing' appoggiatura from one note to another, complete with an illusion of diminuendo:

Ex. 4

Listen attentively to the release of the first note as well as to the attack of the second. Determine in terms of the instrument and the room's acoustics how soon that release must occur to produce the desired effect.

Only after the legato touch has been completely conquered ought we to venture to increase the interval between two notes so as to detach them more and more. Very gradually, working with just a few notes at a time, we can enlarge our palette of touch to encompass the whole spectrum from legato to staccato.

The basic touch described here, though surely fundamental, is not universal in its application. As soon as more than one note in each hand is to be played simultaneously, it becomes impossible to keep literally to the pure finger stroke. The participation of the hand as a unit unavoidably comes into play. But the result must remain the same: a touch resulting from the application of minimum and controlled muscular force and without added weight.

In time, after concentrating on the basic touch in music which is essentially two-part, one for each hand, we can begin to approach thicker textures. Later on, we shall learn even to play quick successions of chords and octaves without bearing down with the weight of the arm. It is in this respect that harpsichord technique differs most noticeably from that of the pianoforte. The modern piano demands the constant application of weight.

But neither is it a flabby, limp and essentially soft stroke of the finger which is needed on the harpsichord. In playing these first little series of notes, look at your fingers from the side. They should be moving up and down like parts of a precision machine: the pistons of an engine, so to speak.

So much for the five-finger position where the hand remains stationary. The passing of the thumb under the hand or the fingers over the thumb, a technical problem familiar to every pianist, is accomplished in a substantially similar way at the harpsichord. A slight tilting of the forearm to assist the smooth passage is essential but any resulting thrust of weight into the keys must be absolutely avoided. Later, when one has developed a technique sufficient for the virtuoso demands of many Scarlatti sonatas and some of the more taxing Rameau pieces, it will be found that wrist and forearm necessarily have to work in a rotational sense. In such cases, too, we must avoid pushing or thrusting into the keys. What is involved essentially is merely an enlargement of the weightless motions employed in moving from one five-finger position to another.

Those working at two-manual instruments will have noted immediately that the touch on the upper keyboard is somewhat lighter and rather more difficult to control. The weight will have to be less because an upper manual key moves only one or two jacks while the lower keys, which have longer levers for reasons of construction, will often have to work four. (All jacks operated by each manual are always raised by the key vertically. It is only their lateral positioning that changes when the register is engaged or disengaged.)

In addition to adapting to the slight difference in touch of the upper manual, you may at first find that playing on it continually produces a sense of strain in the muscles of the upper arm and shoulder. These muscles are required to exert themselves much more

than when they merely keep the hand poised over the lower keyboard. The sense of strain will disappear in time, provided one has
been careful not to play too long at a time on the upper manual.
At the least sign of cramp you must at once cease to use the upper
keyboard. If difficulty persists, it may be necessary to raise your
seat slightly to ease the efforts of the muscles concerned.

Shifting from the lower to the upper manual and back again
needs careful preparation and execution of the required motions.
The shorter the keys of each and the closer the level of the keyboards, one to the other, the less actual movement will be needed.
An ascent is prepared by working the hand gradually backwards
(i.e. away from your body and towards the instrument) into the
lower manual keys before the change of keyboard. The descent is
accomplished in the reverse manner, that is by working the hand
forward to the edge of the keys, then down to the lower manual.
But often there will not be time for much preparation, particularly
in fast tempos. The balanced, weightless arm will simply have to
swing like a crane to carry the hand from its position on one keyboard to the other. The three long fingers in the centre of the hand
are usually the most convenient for pivoting when changing from
upper to lower manual. Conversely, the thumb, and occasionally
the little finger, will serve as the pivot for swinging from the lower
to the upper keyboard. Considerable practice will be required to
achieve a weightless descent onto the lower manual, most especially
where the thumb is called upon to begin the new phrase below.

Special exercises can be devised to gain skill in effecting smooth
transitions from keyboard to keyboard. For example, one can take
a simple phrase and divide almost arbitrarily between lower 8-foot
and upper until only the difference in tone-colour remains to show
where the seam really is. One of the most useful types of piece for
more extended practice of this sort are the four Bach duets (BWV
802-805), where artificial division of phrase lengths will no longer
be necessary. On the contrary, the music itself suggests (if it does
not actually dictate) the manual changes within these giant two-part
inventions.

No matter how carefully we listen and however hard we practise,
it will sometimes seem that instead of progressing, we are sliding

back to a lower level of technical skill. For most performers this is an all too familiar experience at the recital and concert level. Small wonder that something similar should arise during the practice stage. Should this be your experience, particularly during the vital process of mastering the basic touch, it may be advisable to turn away from the instrument for a while. The intense concentration that is needed to make practice sessions really count can be more tiring to the mind than we often realise. Many short bursts of truly concentrated effort will often yield more in terms of positive results than excessively long, tedious sessions at the keyboard.

Certainly, the moment attention flags—as soon as the state of the world or of your bank account comes to mind—it is time to stop what is, after all, no longer practice but mere strumming. Individual capacity for giving undivided attention without momentary lapses varies so greatly that no more specific rule can be laid down. A part of the essence of genius seems to reside in the ability to maintain a concentrated attitude for much longer than ordinary men can.

V

TECHNIQUE THROUGH MUSIC

Fortunately the era of the harpsichord with which we are principally concerned ended about 1750, some years before the invention of the étude. Thus we need only direct our attention to the actual musical materials which were used by the harpsichordists themselves for pedagogical purposes. An examination of the available evidence, such as François Couperin's *L'Art de Toucher le Clavecin* among the few early methods, and the information that has come down to us about J. S. Bach's teaching practices, shows that, apart from a few special technical exercises—principally scales, arpeggios and ornaments—they began with the use of simple pieces. These were almost solely two-part pieces at the start. Only gradually did the texture become more complex.

Two-part keyboard music is much more than mere pabulum for beginners. Entire recital programmes of two-part works in larger forms could be constructed with great taste and sophistication, drawing only on works of the great masters. The singular value of two-part compositions for the student is that they permit the greatest possible attention both to touch and to the detailed articulation and phrasing of each part.

The especial musical virtue of instruments such as the harpsichord and the classical organ resides in their ability to express with utter clarity and perfection of line the vertical structure of music made up of horizontal elements. This they can accomplish even if all the parts are played in one timbre or at one dynamic level at the same time. But these instruments, on the other hand, are not inherently suited to presenting the inner structure and meaning of a musical phrase to the listener by varying timbre and dynamic intensity within it. Some harpsichordists have chosen to overlook this; they play the instrument as if it were a kind of plucked pianoforte. By incessant manipulation of pedals, a variety of artificial and forced nuances can be extracted from the modern instrument by registration alone. Fortunately that tendency is now in its decline.

How these aesthetic considerations should be related to the technique of the harpsichord, and how technique can be acquired from repertoire pieces may not be immediately apparent. Yet what better way to learn to make music in the best sense than by concentrating with complete intensity on learning how to articulate a musical line with the greatest degree of nuance? The illusion of varying timbre and dynamic intensity is one of the effects created by such a nuanced articulation of the musical line on the harpsichord. The two-part approach through actual music, through having real pieces to perform, is the soundest way to attain this special skill.

But acquiring a technique at the harpsichord cannot quite be limited to musical works of progressive difficulty alone. Some purely technical work of very limited scope is also needed. At one time in the history of piano pedagogy, far too much was made of the practice of scales and arpeggios by the hour and in myriad variations. It is now recognised that the essential value of practising these patterns lies in the simple fact that so much music is made up of them.

For exactly that reason—a scale in Scarlatti is technically no different from one in Beethoven—the reader would do well to transfer his previous experience and facility to his new instrument by devoting part of his daily practice to the usual major, minor and chromatic scales and a selection of arpeggios. But that must be done within the framework of the basic touch. Particular attention should be paid to the graceful and easy passage of the thumb with the aid of gentle but weightless rotational motions of the wrist and arm. Remember that their function is to poise and balance and so position the hand and fingers. No thumping on the keys should be permitted. The noiseless quality of one's touch can be checked by occasional playing on the keyboard with all registers disengaged. On most double harpsichords this can be carried a step further: a visual check can also be made by silencing both keyboards and playing on the lower with the coupler engaged.

In earlier times the special study of ornaments, trills above all, was considered essential technical training. This study was never cultivated to nearly the same extent on the pianoforte as was the drilling of scales and arpeggios into the student's head and hands. Yet, how few pianists have we heard who command a full range of trills, at all speeds and dynamic levels? All too often it has been thought that by attaining a swiftness in the alternation of two tones approximating that of a telephone bell, the ultimate in artistic refinement has been attained. The harpsichordist in particular must be able to play short trills and long ones, fast trills and slow ones, trills constant in speed and trills which accelerate or even decelerate as they proceed. But as will be seen in the chapter on ornaments further on, there is an immense range of expressive power in each form of ornament, not merely trills alone. From the very start, whether played initially in a 'correct' form or not, all ornaments that appear in even the simplest pieces should be realised in an expressive and not merely mechanical way.

Before practising the trill, begin by examining the hand. As a rule it is those pairs of fingers, not necessarily adjacent ones, which are most nearly alike in length which will produce the most even and technically perfect trill. But we should make every effort to learn to play the best possible trill with all the other pairs of fingers, too, for ornaments in actual music do not always occur in convenient positions. Unless one's little finger is rather long, for example, it is unlikely that its trill with the neighbouring ring finger will ever be a source of great pride. But that is no reason for not doing all that one can to improve it.

Trilling with non-adjacent fingers, thumb and middle, index and ring, middle and little, is often easier since a slight rotational element can be introduced. But the emphasis should be put on finger action even in these quasi-rotational trills. By trilling alternately with adjacent and non-adjacent pairs of fingers one can learn to maintain an essentially finger-based stroke. For harpsichordists it is unwise to rely solely on the side-to-side rocking of the hand when trilling with non-adjacent fingers as pianists often can.

Learning to change fingers easily in the course of a trill has another important virtue. Trills often end with a turn and even where they do not, one frequently has to prepare the hand at the end of a prolonged trill for what is to follow. Some players find that a long trill can be maintained at speed more easily if fingers are changed, either in a regular pattern or after the initial pair of fingers tires.

Here are a few trill exercises that should be worked through on all degrees of the scale with all pairs of adjacent and non-adjacent fingers, using both naturals and sharps of the keyboard.

Ex. 5

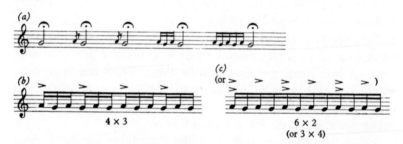

But the greatest technical lessons of all will be learnt through the perfection of every piece studied, from the simplest to the most complex. If you are going to study by yourself without a teacher, it is an excellent plan to set yourself certain goals, to be reached by a certain time, as if you had to perform a particular piece for a teacher or an audience at that point. The tape recorder can also be invaluable as a check on what you really play.

The choice of pieces to be undertaken at the start of your work at the harpsichord is very great. Lists could be offered giving specific works to be studied in a prescribed order but they would fail to take into account the musical experience and preferences of the individual player. The emphasis already placed on two-part music suggests, obviously, that an early goal for study should be the *Two-Part Inventions* of Bach. So they should be, but not to the exclusion of some of the simpler duets for two hands, so to speak, by other composers. The works of Purcell, Rameau, Handel and Scarlatti, for instance, all offer many such pieces.

VI

FINGERING

Wanda Landowska's gift for turning a phrase was not limited to the keyboard. One of her neatest epigrams was her statement that 'fingering is the strategy of the hands'. Indeed, the choice of a fingering on the harpsichord is of vital and far-reaching importance, but unlike fingering on the piano, it does not have specific dynamic implications. We all recall, for instance, that a little extra push or weight was needed to compensate for the relative weakness of the ring finger at the piano. On other occasions we may have used the ring finger purposely to give a particular note lesser sonority.

On the harpsichord, of course, such reinforcement by weight would be counter-productive, as we have seen. The pressure required to depress a harpsichord key, even if it has five or six jacks to lift, should not as a rule strain the capacities of even the weakest of fingers. The real importance of fingering lies in its dual rôle of aiding the harpsichordist first, in achieving a proper inflection of the musical line through articulation and phrasing, and second, in preparing the hand to move from one position to another.

There is considerable historical evidence on the matter of fingering, some of it going back as far as the sixteenth century. In general, the fingerings in use down to the time of Bach and Couperin were characterised by a tendency to avoid the use of the extreme outer fingers, the thumb and little finger—except in sixths and octaves, large chords, and at the beginning or end of phrases. The thumb as a multiplier of the fingers, as a pivot over which they pass or as something which moves under them to relocate the hand, was largely ignored until the early eighteenth century. Modern piano fingering really came into its own only in the period from Clementi to Chopin and has even been modified since.

In various works suggested for further reading in Chapter XIV, the reader may learn in detail how the sixteenth-century Italians and Spaniards fingered their pieces, what John Bull's and other virginalists' fingerings were like, what Couperin and the other clavecinistes taught, and what we know of J. S. Bach's fingerings from the two fully-fingered pieces in the *Clavierbüchlein für Wilhelm Friedemann*—one in the 'old style', the other in the modern.

But I believe it would be idle, even foolish, for the modern harpsichordist, particularly one trained at the pianoforte, to return dogmatically to the fingerings of earlier times. Moreover, the fingering system of, say, the English virginalists would not be appropriate, or even adequate for music of the eighteenth century. To master all these systems is clearly out of the question. Also, we have no significant information about the fingerings of many important keyboard masters such as Froberger, Handel and Scarlatti, to name but three. What is important for the modern performer of their music is to recognise what the earlier types of fingering were intended to achieve and then produce the same musical effects with more modern fingerings.

The older fingerings yielded a very expressive, highly articulated musical line, one composed of the linking of many short groupings of notes, two, three and four at a time. The more extended groupings, whether in a legato or semi-detached *jeu perlé*, which we find in late eighteenth- and nineteenth-century piano music, are rarely if ever encountered in earlier works. Pieces that appear to us as made up of such long groupings, notably works of the virginalists, will never give up their secrets to us unless we play them in a more articulated and finely inflected style. Occasionally there are lines which must be heard in one dash along the keyboard, particularly scales such as these found in Handel:

Ex. 6   Handel, Variation 5 from Suite, No. 5, Air and Variations

and Scarlatti:

Ex. 7   D. Scarlatti, Sonata, K.406 (L.5)

But these are very late examples. Besides, it would be quite erroneous
to turn Handel's variations on a kind of gavotte into a giddy race
to the finish at the final cadence or to play the Scarlatti sonata so
quickly as to make the scale figure sound like the tearing of a piece
of cloth.

Two devices characteristic of older fingerings are of special
practical importance to the harpsichordist: the crossing of long
fingers, index, middle and ring, one over the other, somewhat in
the manner of Chopin's étude in *A* minor, op. 10, no. 2 and the silent
substitution of one finger for another to permit repositioning the

Ex. 8   Chopin, Etude, Op. 10, No. 2

(Chopin's fingering)

Ex. 9   F. Couperin, Les Ondes, 5th Ordre

(Couperin's fingering)

hand. This latter device was in fact claimed by François Couperin as his own invention when he wrote his harpsichord method.

Ex. 10   F. Couperin, Prelude, *No. 1*

It is impossible to perform much polyphonic keyboard music without recourse to silent finger changes.

Ex. 11   J. S. Bach, Fugue, *No. 9, W.T.C. II (BMV 878)*

Yet there are times when it will be found equally practicable, and perhaps even preferable, to shift the entire hand in a manner more often associated with the keyboard music of Brahms than Bach.

Ex. 12   J. S. Bach, Overture, *Partita, No. 4 (BMV 828)*

As always, one must try the alternative solutions in all doubtful cases. In no event should the entire hand be shifted if that results in an awkward thump or lack of rhythmical continuity. Remember that the harpsichord does not offer the resources of the damper pedal to paper over the cracks.

Correct fingering is never the result of random factors, the product of pure chance. Rather, it always must be arrived at through conscious, rational choice amongst available alternatives. Certain patterns, like those of a scale, become so ingrained that the choice is predetermined. But most passages will require some considerable thought and musical analysis before a particular fingering will present itself as the one of choice. What is meant here by 'musical analysis' will be examined in further detail below. Suffice it to say here that no fingering should ever be selected solely for motives of convenience. Every fingering must be chosen in the first instance because it is the one best suited for the realisation of a musical objective, that is, performing the passage in question in the way which one feels to be musically satisfying.

The playing of more than one part in each hand, that is the performance of double-note passages in polyphonic music, usually entails a division of the hand into two separate parts, one composed of the thumb and the index finger, the other of the remaining three fingers. The former part, thanks largely to scale practice and the skill thus acquired in passing over and under the thumb, will probably have been developed to a higher degree of agility than the other part with its one 'strong' and two 'weak' fingers.

In seeking out fingerings for passages which involve such a splitting of the hand into two halves, each line should be studied separately using only the fingers of the part concerned. The other fingers should be held in a relaxed but alert state without any stiffness or tension. First the inner part then the outer part should be played in steady alternation until they can be ventured as a whole. Such an approach is actually far less tedious than trying to find a solution by incessant repetition of the whole, only to find after a hundred fumbling attempts, that the passage defies you still.

A related fine point of fingering involves the connexion of those individual notes in a single melodic line which must be divided between the hands. Inner voices are constantly passing from left to right and back again. The thumb, a strong but clumsy digit, bears the major burden of this delicate task. Not only will thumb frequently follow thumb in the sequence of the fingering, but on occasion the only way to deal gracefully with a passage is for the inner voice to be passed back and forth continually.

Ex. 13   J. S. Bach, Sinfonia, *No. 3 (BWV 789)*

Repeated notes pervade the repertoire from the virginalists and Sweelinck down to those sonatas of Scarlatti with effects which recall the mandolin, drums and even castanets.

Ex. 14   Sweelinck, Variation 3, Mein Junges Leben

The immediate question that arises in each such passage is whether to change fingers or repeat notes with the same finger. The answer will depend on several factors. Very quick repetitions like the beating of a drum will usually sound best with changing fingers.

Ex. 15   D. Scarlatti, Sonata, K.435 (L.361)

Slower, more expressive uses of repeated notes can often be articulated less mechanically by keeping the same finger at work. The
fingerings indicated above in Exx. 14 and 15 illustrate this difference
in musical intent, and how the choice of fingering relates to it. One
special note for pianists is in order here. Those who have learnt to
play on modern grands with a double escapement action may find
the action of even the best harpsichord troublesome in regard to
repeated notes. Unlike the Erard double-escapement action used in
grand pianos, which allows a note to be restruck before the key has
come all the way back to its original level, the harpsichord key
must return to the top or within a hair's breadth of it in order to
repeat. But this is not at all disadvantageous because proper damping, essential to making the point of the repetition clear, especially
in the case of quick ones, requires such a return of the key. Furthermore, the harpsichord's key dip is less than that of the piano. On a
well-made and properly regulated harpsichord action it will always
be possible to play as quickly as the music needs to be performed,
including repeated notes, trills and all the other tests of an action's
efficiency.

VII

ANALYSIS AND SYNTHESIS

Having now disposed of some basic technical aspects of playing the harpsichord, let us turn to a consideration of how a piece of music as such may best be studied. No novelty is claimed for the method advocated here, but it can at least be reduced to a pair of maxims: know your music well; and learn one thing at a time. In these apparently trite exhortations resides the secret of effective study.

Knowing your music well means that you must first analyse it. How often have you actually studied a composition before sitting down to try it at the keyboard for the first time? If you attempt to analyse it at all, do you not do this more often later on, when your curiosity has been aroused or, as is more frequent, when special difficulties have been encountered?

The degree to which prior analysis can be carried out depends on your powers of concentration and, to some extent, on your sense of musical logic and form, quite apart from formal theoretical training.

You may be familiar with the most extreme development of this approach in the teaching of some famous piano pedagogues who demand that a piece should be completely committed to memory before a single note of it may be played by the student! That rule is perhaps impractical, possibly even cruel, considering that the purpose of playing an instrument includes giving some joy to oneself. But without laying down any such absolute precondition, I still believe that most inaccuracies in performance, the majority of the slips and stumbles which mar the playing of many non-professionals particularly, arise because a musician does not know his music intimately. Thus conflicts are born, such as, 'do I play this note or that', which, in turn, produce tension, physical as well as mental, leading to technical and interpretative calamities.

To avoid these conflicts and tensions we must see to it that they do not arise in the first place. The challenge of each piece must be met by careful analysis. To make such an analysis does not mean that you must be able to translate into technical language everything that happens in the music; that may be left to the theoretician. Rather, the analysis must meet two simple criteria: first, the conscious recognition of every significant event in the music, and second, the relating of each such happening to the other events in the piece. In other words, we must constantly be asking what is happening and whether it is the same or different from what has gone before. Once we are clear about that much, we are well on our way to mastering the piece.

Few of us who are not thoroughly trained musicians can claim to hear music in our minds merely by reading the notes. Keyboard players find that quite hard where music for their instruments is concerned. They immediately set their fingers in motion and finally dash to the nearest keyboard to give sound and meaning to the vague mental image of what is implied by the printed page. The ability to read music and hear it mentally must be developed through practice. Not only will that relieve us of much of the tedium of incessant repetitions at the keyboard, to the great relief of our neighbours if not ourselves, but it will enable us to practise with our minds even when an instrument is not at hand.

In addition, we should understand the music we play in terms of song and dance. The secret of phrasing and rhythm very often lies in humming a part of a work under study, singing over a bar or two, even whistling a snatch of it. Similarly we can sometimes decipher a rhythmically obscure passage by dancing or at least moving our bodies in some way related to the flow of the music.

Now, what are the significant events in a piece of music? The catalogue is certainly a long one, even for relatively simple works— the more so since it must embrace not only the smallest details but also the features of its basic structure, the skeletal anatomy of the piece, as it were. To begin with, it is well to survey the work as a whole and block out its general form. Does it fall clearly into three sections like so many pavans and galliards, for example, or into two, like the dances used in the suite and the sonatas of Domenico Scarlatti?

It will be found that, except for pieces in variation form, certain fugal and imitative pieces and the more extended types of rondo, virtually every composition can be divided, at least superficially, into two or three main sections, often with double bars to make the matter completely obvious.

Occasionally there are ambiguities, of course, even in the overall design. Should one, for example, repeat the *première partie* after the *seconde partie* of certain Couperin pieces although they both end on the tonic of their common key? Couperin does not tell us to do so but perhaps our musical instinct and analysis do. Does a particular dominant-tonic succession rank as an important cadence of structural significance or is it just a halt en route to something more important?

Once the overall structure has been blocked out, you can then begin to pick out the themes or subjects. Which is the first one? How often, where and in what form does it recur? What happens to it rhythmically and harmonically? And so on, through the entire piece with each element as it occurs and recurs. The entire exercise is similar to what we may have been trained to do in analysing a poem or a painting. It is really a kind of stocktaking but it holds the clue to perceiving a work as anything more than a mere stringing together of unrelated events. How these events are identified in terms of labels is unimportant. It is the fact of their being both recognised and mentally labelled which counts.

After preparing the inventory you can proceed to consider some further details. What sort of tempo is called for? What do the ornament signs mean? Why do the signs come when they do and for what musical purpose? Are there places where some free ornamentation or other filling-out of the written notes seems appropriate or essential? What technical features of the piece need special working out at the keyboard? What does the texture of various sections suggest in terms of registration? Is the piece to be played on a single dynamic level or on two—or even more? How could this have been dealt with on the instruments of the time and place of composition?

All the mind's telescopes and microscopes can be brought into play during this examination. The more the work can be examined in detail, even just in the sense of mentally noting every discernible feature and potential difficulty, the better prepared we shall be to play it—easily, confidently, knowingly. What is more, there is a clear benefit in terms of transferability of experience. The tenth Bach fugue studied in this way will be far simpler than the first. The tenth, in turn, will illuminate the first still further.

Most, though not all, performers feel a sense of freedom and confidence when they are liberated from the printed page. Memorisation has become traditional for pianists but many harpsichordists regularly appear in public with their notes, particularly those originally trained on the organ, an instrument which screens the performer from public view. It is certainly worth making an effort to gain the freedom that memorisation affords the player. Everyone can do so to some degree, be it only four bars a day. The more one does memorise, the more one can. After the kind of analysis we have been discussing, directed to elimination of conflicts in advance, memorising should be all the simpler.

A good way of learning to memorise is to try to get a few bars to stay in your mind. Then place the music in an inaccessible place where it will be out of sight. Next try to reproduce the passage. If it succeeds, well and good; proceed to the next one. If not, go back to the printed notes and try again. Cell by cell, phrase by phrase the process goes forward, with periodic trials of more extended fragments.

Once analysis has progressed beyond the purely morphological aspects of the matter, it is time to combine it with actual work at the keyboard. We are now beginning to know our music well, and it is time to consider the implications of the second basic tenet of the system; learn one thing at a time.

To suggest total resistance to temptation at this point would be to ask too much. It is very useful, in fact, to confirm or at least check the accuracy of our work by playing the whole piece through once or twice from the notes. Next, play it through once more but stopping at each problem, taking careful note of the difficulty if it involves more than a mere lapse in the reading of the notes. Mark these well both in your mind and on the page.

In the case of an invention or fugue, for example, the approach to be used is clear: learn each voice in all its aspects, but only in a musical sense not a technical one for the moment. Concentrate on the melodic and rhythmic features of the part. Imagine it really is a vocal part, sing it if you can, and note where you think breath should be taken. This will immediately illuminate the articulation and phrasing of the line; in other words, which elements in it should be connected and which should be detached. When each part has been thoroughly learnt—that is, can be played in a completely articulated and phrased manner—then it is time to combine the parts, noting particularly the opposition of rhythms in the various voices.

It is during the working out of the combined parts that you can begin to think about the choice of fingerings. In essence the task consists in seeing to it that no element in the articulation and phrasing of any one part is sacrificed by its combination with the other parts. Fingerings must always be responsive first of all to the musical requirements and not to mere convenience. We may have to modify some details because they are no longer appropriate when the parts are put together.

To give continuity to one's work, since practice hours are limited, it is essential to mark the music to show what has been decided at each session. Pencils being generally provided with rubbers as well as leads, we can make way for wisdom even if it should come to us late. It is in no sense a defeat—indeed it is a triumph—if, after conscientious practice of a passage, you see it in a new and different light and decide to erase earlier markings in favour of new ones.

For pieces written in a homophonic texture, like many dance and character pieces, with a clearly defined melodic line in the right hand and an accompaniment in the left, the voice by voice approach must be modified. The tune will actually be studied as if it were one part of a polyphonic work, of course. But the significance of the accompaniment must on no account be underestimated. Its rhythmic functions may even outweigh the harmonic support it affords the melody. The rhythmical inflection of the accompaniment figure is vital to the life of the melodic line above it. Consider for a moment how in the performance of a Chopin mazurka or a Viennese waltz it is the accompaniment that gives the swing, the characteristic lilt, the very life to the piece. So it is, too, in the case of many homophonically conceived harpsichord pieces, especially so when the accompaniment consists of a repeated chordal figure, either in block form or broken into some pattern such as an Alberti bass. A slight delay of the downbeat may be needed in the case of a Scarlatti sonata:

Ex. 16   D. Scarlatti, Sonata, *K.29 (L.461)*

The subtle trace of rubato achieved by a lingering on the downbeat played precisely in time is required at other times:

Ex. 17   F. Couperin, Rondeau, Les Bergeries, *6th Ordre*

On other occasions, a completely mechanical precision will be appropriate:

Ex. 18   F. Couperin, Rondeau, Le Tic-Toc-Choc, 18th Ordre

Learning one thing at a time means exactly that. With a rhythmical problem, for instance, it is best to isolate it from the context and to solve it in its pure form. Beat out the time values with a finger or a pencil. This should be too obvious to require mention; but all too often the student simply persists in a frontal assault on the whole complex of which the rhythmic difficulty is but one part. If an ornament seems beyond one's capacity, for example one of Couperin's troublesome turned shakes in the left hand, it can be

Ex. 19   F. Couperin, Rondeau, Les Moissonneurs, 6th Ordre

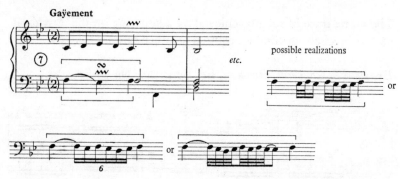

attacked as a special technical problem. A fingering can be worked out which puts the least strain on the hand and allows both a graceful trill and a final turn to be played gracefully. You must also decide exactly how many repercussions are called for; often what is attempted is not only difficult but actually less tasteful. By transforming the fragment of the piece temporarily into an exercise, you can transpose it to other parts of the keyboard with various combinations of naturals and sharps. Finally, the fragment can be put back into its original context, and when you confirm that it can now be played, you will have moved one step farther along the road to mastering the piece.

The tape recorder, even in its simplest and least costly form, has already been mentioned as a most valuable means of checking the accuracy of one's own listening. But it is not a substitute for the sharply focused aural attention on which musicians have always had to rely. By playing back at half- or even quarter-speed, however, tapes can be used in a way that cannot be matched by the unaided ear, or that of a teacher. Not that every practice session ought to be recorded—by no means. But the critical passages can be checked with incredible accuracy through tapes. Similarly the smallest details of recorded performances can be examined under a time-lens, so to speak, by tape analysis: articulations, ornaments, rhythmical alterations, all the finest nuances which result from the careful timing of attacks and releases.

By now, the precepts of knowing the music well and learning one thing at a time, should no longer appear so bromidic. When you consider how much there is to know about the simplest little minuet, respect grows immeasurably greater for even competent, let alone inspired performances of great works.

Remember, too, that it is easier to learn than to unlearn. No mistake should be allowed to pass uncorrected. Mark every point in the music which gives rise to doubt or conflict, particularly passages which are almost alike but not quite.

Each time you sit down at the harpsichord, you should do so in full awareness of why you are there. If the immediate purpose is one of study—to perfect the fingering of a passage or to work out its ornaments, to verify the steadiness of a tempo with the metronome or to sight-read a piece which you propose to learn—then only study is proper. If, on the other hand, you are about to perform, whether for an audience or merely for yourself, then the mind must be swept clean of petty details and all concentration directed towards the long line of the music, the large units of the form, the major features of the piece. A balance between the two approaches, the intensive and the extensive, between study and performance will help to keep both deficiencies and progress properly in perspective.

And if occasionally, when you probably ought to be polishing fine details you instead decide to play the harpsichord for the sheer fun of it, for the joy of making music, for the sake of relaxation, it would take a heart of stone not to extend some measure of sympathy to such an eminently pardonable human weakness.

VIII

ARTICULATION AND PHRASING

Because of the harpsichord's basic inability to play one note louder than another, it is vital to compensate for this dynamic rigidity by the most careful attention to articulation. Our object must be to mould the musical line, to shape it into perceptible form so that each musical section of it audibly begins, develops and concludes. To this end we can determine which notes shall sound earlier or later, longer or shorter, and which shall be connected to or detached from the notes which precede or follow them. That has already been emphasised in the section dealing with technique since, in striving for good articulation, the means and the ends are inseparable. The ability to play any given note patterns—scales, arpeggios, and the like—at any prescribed speed is musically valueless unless we can simultaneously control the timing and the relative degree of connexion of the notes. It holds true for other instruments. But all of them, save only the classical organ, have at their disposal the additional factor of dynamic stress.

Articulation is commonly compared to punctuation whilst phrasing is said to resemble the division of prose of the pre-Joycean variety into sentences and paragraphs. Thus, articulation properly refers to the long or short, connected or detached, qualities of shorter groups of notes which make up the smallest perceptible units of the musical line. Phrasing is the term we use primarily to denote the interspersion of miniscule silences, breaks, breathing spaces—between what in music corresponds to sentences and paragraphs or to their constituent words and clauses—that is, between the small units referred to in the preceding sentences, whether taken individually or in groups.

But in any musical phrase made up of several bars there are both heavy and light ones, just as within a single bar there will be heavy and light beats. Some phrases will have to be detached from those that follow them in a much more pronounced, sharp manner than would otherwise be appropriate. At times phrases will occur which overlap; both will be perceptible as discrete units, but the end of the first will also mark the beginning of the second.

The rhythmical counterpoint of differently articulated but simultaneous lines enlivens harpsichord music quite as much as the interplay of consonant and dissonant combinations of sounds. To achieve such rhythmical counterpoints composers are often at pains to ensure that the phrase lengths of different voices of a polyphonic work coincide only at certain points but not throughout an entire piece. If the phrases of each voice always began and ended together the effect would be very much like that produced by the singing of a chorale or a hymn: solid, four-square, and often monotonous.

What does this mean in practice? The essential task of a musical performance is two-fold. It must both make clear the form of the whole piece and at the same time set off each detail in appropriate relief. Possibly the best comparison one could make would be to a Japanese scroll painting. Each element of the scroll relates to what precedes and what follows it. Yet throughout one has a sense of the entire work.

In contrapuntal works, it is wise to ponder the structure of the themes, clearly identifying the elements of a fugue subject, since these recur in various guises throughout the piece. Very often the episodes between successive workings-out of the fugue subject are built out of little fragments of the subject developed and put to new and different uses. Note, too, whether any articulation signs or ornaments appear in the first statement of any theme. Often those signs have to be entered at the subsequent appearances of the same theme. Composers were notoriously lazy about writing them out more than once. Bach, for example, in some of the fugues of the *Forty-Eight* only indicated essential markings of articulation and ornamentation at the first statement of the subject:

Ex. 20   J. S. Bach, *Fugue, No. 22, W.T.C. II (BWV 891)*

Ex. 21   J. S. Bach, *Fugue, No. 12, W.T.C. II (BWV 881)*

Probably the most treacherous traps in harpsichord music are those involving the repetition of identical material. We should pay careful attention to such repeated figures, and even whole bars or groups of them. Some are meant to sound as literal repetitions; others are not. The false tradition of the 'automatic echo' in performing the sonatas of Scarlatti grew out of such a failure to distinguish between real and apparent repetitions. In terms of articulation alone, there is much that can be done to emphasise or minimise the sameness, or occasionally even shade the degree of connexion or detachment, and produce an equivalent intensification or abatement of the musical line. What does an actor do when faced with lines such as Lear must declaim in Act V, Scene 3? It would be unthinkable to pronounce each of these repeated words identically:

'No, no, no, no! Come, let's away to prison . . .'   (8)
'Howl, howl, howl, howl! O, you are men of stones . . .' (257)
'Never, never, never, never, never!'   (308)

Nothing will make our playing more tedious than bland repetition, unrelieved by shadings of articulation, each time seemingly identical patterns are repeated verbatim.

By analogy with vocal music, conjunct lines (where the notes move up or down a single step at a time) tend to be legato, smoothly connected. Disjunct lines, unless taken at a considerable speed, rather tend to be detached. Like all generalisations this is subject to many exceptions but it will serve as a point of departure in considering what articulations are likely to fit a particular line. The wider the interval, the greater the probability that detachment is appropriate. Note, however, that detachment does not necessarily mean staccato, an extreme shortening of duration. As mentioned in the treatment of the basic harpsichord touch, very short staccatos, familiar in piano music such as a Mendelssohn scherzo, are usually ineffective and unstylistic on the harpsichord.

IX

RHYTHM AND TEMPO

Underlying the articulated lines and phrased segments of the music is the metre—the regular and recurrent pulsations, two, three, four or more beats which make up each bar, as indicated by the time signature. Imposed upon the metre is rhythm, the irregular groupings of beats which result from the musical line, written inside the framework of a given metre.

Thus, for example, the sarabandes of Bach's D minor and G major *French Suites* are both written in the same $\frac{3}{4}$ metre but the rhythm of each is entirely different:

Ex. 22   J. S. Bach, Sarabande, French Suite, *No. 1 (BWV 812)*

Ex. 23   J. S. Bach, Sarabande, French Suite, *No. 5 (BWV 816)*

Yet, common to both sarabandes, is the balance struck between grace and gravity. The player must distinguish clearly between strong and weak beats (which are not always the first and subsequent beats of a bar) in order to bring out the underlying rhythm. The clicking of a metronome is not rhythmical but only metrical, and makes no distinction between strong and weak beats. But weak beats in themselves can also serve as upbeats to strong ones. Note how the last beat of a bar in particular is often rushed over by performers so as to allow the strong downbeat to arrive too soon. One should pay very special attention to these last beats and their subdivisions, both for their own sakes and, even more important, to ensure giving the ensuing downbeat its proper due.

The three superimposed elements of metre, rhythm and articulation plus the sub-division of the music by phrasing together make what is generally termed 'rhythm' in laymen's parlance. In harpsichord music, just as in jazz, the 'beat' results from the interaction of all these elements.

The speed with which these and the other components of the music can best be perceived in their relationships to each other represents the ideal tempo of a piece. One also has to take into account the shape of the melodic line as well as the consonance-dissonance interplay which lends harmonic interest to the music. Added to these internal factors are external ones that are no less material. The resonance of the room and of the instrument are important determinants of tempo. We all know that four or five voices singing in a small hall packed to the rafters can take a much faster tempo than a large chorus rehearsing the same piece in an empty Albert Hall. A dramatic soprano will usually have to move her voice at a slower pace than another singer with a small, silvery and accordingly flexible vocal instrument.

Physiological factors, too, play an important part in determining tempos. What is a 'normal' pulse or breathing rate? The range can be quite broad. The different tempos taken by equally great musicians in performing the same piece must surely derive in no small measure from just such factors. Otherwise how should we account for some of the more extreme cases?

The classical harpsichord repertory, of course, contains no authentic metronome markings and composers often did not even consider it necessary to indicate tempos at all. Bach's *Italian Concerto*, for instance, has andante and presto as the tempos of its second and third movements but the opening movement must have seemed so obviously to require an allegro tempo that the composer did not label it at all. But what does allegro mean in any case? The word originally had connotations of happiness rather than anything suggesting speed, as even English-speaking countries know from their Milton. Not every indication of allegro is by any means to be taken as signifying a very fast tempo. Scarlatti uses the word in his sonatas more frequently than any other. He must have had quite a range of possibilities in mind. Both of the following are marked allegro:

Ex. 24   D. Scarlatti, Sonata, *K.27 (L.495)*

Ex. 25   D. Scarlatti, Sonata, *K.44 (L.432)*

One is obviously to be taken much more slowly than the other.

Attempts were made in earlier times to make tempos a matter of precision rather than guesswork. But when we examine some of these attempts, such as Loulié's 'chronomètre', a pendulum affair used as a crude metronome at the end of the seventeenth century, or Quantz's attempt to systematise tempos based on a man's 'normal' pulse of eighty beats to the minute, we are quite astounded. Those dignified French chaconnes, for example, whisk along at a hundred and twenty crotchets to the minute, at the slowest. Minuets fly by at quite incredible rates. The difference between our thinking and theirs in respect of tempo is usually far greater than any disagreement which might take place today between two musicians discussing the tempo of a piece of music of the standard repertoire.

If there is all this confusion, how do musicians solve the problem of fixing a tempo? To some extent they are influenced by physical factors in that they are consciously or unknowingly affected by their pulses and breathing rates. And they solve it in part by relating what they play to the sense of physical music-making expressed through song. Because much music of the instrumental type is essentially unsingable, though, substitutes have been devised: simple ones like the 'tum-ti-tum-tum' sort of thing we all invent on occasion, or more sophisticated methods, like the French rhythmical solfège syllables. That is how we voice the unvocal.

Another form of direct physical participation in musical activity is the dance. When we dance we feel the metre and rhythm of the dance in a physical way, conditioned by the speed of our pulse and breathing. Note, too, that as soon as dance pieces cease to be written for dancing but to be played as abstract music, tempos change radically. Chopin's opus 34 includes both an *A* minor waltz far too slow for dancing and an *F* major waltz much too fast to be danced. The tempi of sarabandes and other dances varied in a similar manner.

Finally there is another physical factor to be kept in mind: the acuity of the listener's ears and nervous system. This is a matter of profound importance to the harpsichordist because his instrument lends itself to being played at very high speeds. It is quite possible to play music on it faster than any listener can possibly perceive it, let alone listen to it intelligently, with understanding and enjoyment. There have been harpsichordists who specialise in this sort of performance. Sometimes the underlying attitude may be, 'look at *me*!' rather than, 'look at Scarlatti!' But the motive may be neither meretricious nor malicious in fact. All of us who drive motor cars know how different a sense of speed the driver may have as compared with his passengers. The contact of the body with the steering wheel and pedals of a car can be compared to the physical contact between the performer and his instrument. By dint of great effort of concentration, you can hear as a listener even while you are the performer. Fortunately, we can also use tape recorders to check our tempos, both as to speed and steadiness.

Having now considered articulation, phrasing, rhythm and tempo, we must turn to the ultimate question of how, having once satisfactorily accounted for each of these elements, we can weld them into a unified musical structure. The standard literature for harpsichord, while it includes many extended compositions, does not contain any single movements of uninterrupted flow that extend more than some eight to ten minutes each. The more extended suites and sets of variations can last much longer. Bach's D major partita, for instance, takes over half an hour with repeats, while his *Goldberg Variations* last three times as long if played in full, and every repeat is observed. But those are exceptional works. No single movement runs to the heavenly lengths of the Romantics.

The final fusion of details, deciding the relative importance of each and the emphasis to be placed on it in the overall structure, is in the last analysis a matter of striking a balance. On the one hand we are concerned that the flow of the music, the unfurling of the scroll, should not cease, while on the other, we must see to it that no significant finer point is overlooked. The greater the work, the less the likelihood that we will ever feel that we have actually realised the ideal. Making music at the harpsichord really begins when, after exploring to the full all the conscious elements of the pieces, you pass beyond that stage and confidently allow enlightened instinct to take command. In sum, there is a time to analyse, a time to synthesise, and finally, a time to put all that out of your mind and concentrate exclusively on the sheer joy of making music.

X

ORNAMENTS
AND ORNAMENTATION

Let us begin by stating the basic principles which underlie all that follows. Ornaments are specific embellishments, indicated by signs or shorthand symbols which composers have used in various ways at different times and places. The extent to which composers relied on these symbols varied. Some, like Couperin, were quite explicit, while others, like Cabezón, gave no hint whatever to the performer of what we know from other evidence was, nonetheless, expected of him.

Ornamentation, however, is a much broader concept. Ultimately it can be said to embrace all written-out figurations and passage work, the embellishments indicated by ornament symbols, and the free decoration which the intelligent and sensitive player was expected and, indeed, obliged to provide.

Ornamentation is virtually as old as music itself, for it is found in all but the most primitive forms of the art. As soon as the composer and the performer became separate personalities, each was placed under separate and distinct obligations to decorate the musical line. In the music of our own time, except for improvisatory elements in jazz and certain *avant-garde* music, the composer has assumed the entire burden of decoration. The performer acquits himself of his entire obligation, we are told by such eminent twentieth-century masters as Ravel and Stravinsky, by exact and literal execution of the notes and directions on the printed page. But it was not ever thus—certainly not during the era of the classical harpsichord repertoire.

Like all musical devices, ornamentation has its primary roots in vocal music which, in turn, derives from the artistic use of speech, from declamation. From a study of counterpoint as it evolved during and after the Middle Ages, we know that ornamentation in polyphonic music is closely linked to the artistic use of dissonance. In purely monophonic music—a single musical line—ornamentation can serve expressive as well as purely decorative purposes.

Thus, one function of musical embellishment has been to achieve the desired balance between tension and relaxation through softening or emphasising dissonances.

What does all this ancient history have to do with ornamentation in the performance of harpsichord music? Simply this: the emphasis in all writings on the subject, both those of earlier times and recent ones, has been on formulas. In other words, glossaries have been prepared explaining how particular symbols were to be translated into sound. Other texts have also dealt with free ornamentation as an aspect both of performance and of composition. Most recent writings, for all their merits, have generally limited themselves to collecting, collating and cataloguing the shorthand symbols into a kind of dictionary for the use of performers.

Valuable as they are, these compendia somehow convey the impression that the realisation of the symbols, the actual musical effects they are intended to achieve, are far more standardised than is actually the case. This has at times led to rigidity of performance and a lack of variety in fine detail. The decorations seem no longer to be individually hand-crafted but mass-produced. The results are often inartistic and unconvincing, or as Mme. Landowska put it so well: 'an ornament badly played is like a smile in a toothless mouth'.

What has been lacking is the express recognition of what every musician knows or should know: that in addition to knowing the literally correct interpretation of ornaments, we must also understand their melodic, rhythmic, and harmonic functions. In other words, not only must we ask ourselves, 'what does this ornamental symbol mean in terms of notes?'; but also, 'why is this ornament where it is?' These are questions which properly apply to every instrument. For harpsichordists they are especially important because of the instrument's dynamic limitations. A special additional function of ornamentation of all types in harpsichord music is to belie the fact that the sound is discontinuous. But above all, ornaments and ornamentation are stylistic in their essence.

In addition to enriching the harpsichord's sound, giving it a semblance of cantilena or even just greater fullness of tone, ornaments also can serve a multitude of other purposes. They can be used to accent particular notes, either rhythmically or melodically, to highlight them the way a painter can apply a little fleck of white or a contrasting colour to create a special kind of illusion. They can be used to enliven the musical line, to heighten the mood. They are of particular importance at cadences, at the big full closes as well as at the lesser turns of harmonic phrase which build the tonal structure and outline the form.

In both a sustaining and a melodic sense, ornaments can be used to emphasise an interval gap or, contrariwise, to fill it up, bridging the melodic line to achieve a quasi-legato or portamento effect. Closely allied with this function are the purely expressive ones, the sigh or 'dying fall', the exclamation, the cry of exultation or anger, all of which can be imitated to some degree by the basic undecorated musical line, and even better by the use of the appropriate ornaments.

The sound of other instruments can often be suggested by ornaments, too. The very name 'arpeggio' indicates the derivation of that basic ornamental form from the style and technique of the harp. Scarlatti's repeated notes often suggest the mandolin and its relatives, so much a part of Neapolitan popular music even in his time, or the castanets of the Spain in which he lived for so many years. Drums, bagpipes, bird-calls, all these and more are suggested by the associative use of ornaments in the repertoire of the harpsichord.

Finally, we should also recognise that much ornamentation is employed simply for abstract decorative or 'colour' effects in a quite stylised manner, without specific reference to any express emotional tone or effect, or to any desire to depict something concrete. Much of the formal decoration of French harpsichord music is of this type, or at least can be satisfactorily explained on this basis. This should not be surprising when we reflect for a moment on the prevailing decorative styles in other art forms during the period of the classic harpsichord.

After this brief consideration of the functions of the ornament, it should be clear that the material cannot be neatly systematised into a group of fool-proof formulas, pre-packaged and wrapped in cellophane. But neither should the reader conclude that we are advocating a 'do as you please' solution, or rather, evasion of the problem. Quite the contrary. But where others have suggested that there are 'rules' to be followed, we prefer to deal with them as rebuttable presumptions.

The first presumption is that *all ornaments are to be played on the beat and not before the beat.* Exceptions, and they are relatively few, are noted and explained below. Some are clear on the face of the notation; others can only be inferred from the musical context.

A second such presumption is that *all ornaments, unless expressly indicated to the contrary, should confirm the prevailing tonality and not weaken it.* This is not always an easy principle to apply but the really doubtful cases are fewer than one might think. Consider this fragment from a Bach organ fugue:

Ex. 26   J. S. Bach, Organ Fugue *(BWV 533)*

The mordent over the second note must be played with *A* natural, not *A* sharp, to avoid giving the impression that the piece is in *B* minor (leading note *A* sharp) rather than the actual key, *E* minor. But at the second appearance of the subject, *D* sharp must be used for the mordent to confirm the tonality.

Regardless of the names applied to particular ornaments either in our time or in the past, they can all be classified conveniently under a few headings. It is important to learn how these basic types can be recognised both when written out in normal notation and also in the various forms of abbreviated or symbolic notation used by the composers whose works we study. There is no escaping the task of learning the symbol language of each such composer. Fortunately most of these are fairly uniform within a given period and locale.

But some composers were maddeningly idiosyncratic. Purcell and his followers, for instance, used a sign to denote a mordent which meant a trill to everyone else who used it. Even more troublesome is the general failure to distinguish the kind of passing appoggiatura which is fitted in by stealing a bit of time off the end of the preceding note, from the normal variety which takes part of the value of the following note. Still, there is substantial conformity to certain conventional symbols and the exceptions can soon be learnt.

It is equally perplexing when composers write out some ornamental formulas in full rather than use conventional symbols such as they themselves frequently employ in other situations. Bach, for example, wrote out the mordents in such fugue subjects as:

Ex. 27   J. S. Bach, Fugue, No. 2, W.T.C. I (BWV 847)

Ex. 28   J. S. Bach, Fugue, No. 20, W.T.C. I (BWV 865)

while he did not do so in the organ fugue in Ex. 26. Neither did he use the conventional turn sign in these fugue subjects.

Ex. 29 *J. S. Bach, Fugue, No. 15, W.T.C. I (BWV 860)*

Ex. 30 *J. S. Bach, Fugue, No. 3, W.T.C. I (BWV 848)*

Ex. 31 *J. S. Bach, Fugue, No. 10, W.T.C. II (BWV 879)*

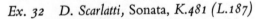

The only reason he could have had for his notation was a wish to prescribe precise realisations and avoid conventional ones which might not achieve quite the same effect.

Similar writings-out characterise the works of other composers, too. Scarlatti, for example, wrote:

Ex. 32 *D. Scarlatti, Sonata, K.481 (L.187)*

rather than use shorthand notation which might have led even the
most sensitive players to perform something like this:

Ex. 33   D. Scarlatti, Sonata, K.481 (L.187)

Some composers consistently avoided using certain symbolic
forms, always preferring to write the ornament out. Scarlatti (despite
Longo's edition) seems never to have used the mordent symbol, but
he often wrote mordents into his music.

Ex. 34   D. Scarlatti, Sonata, K.44 (L.432)

Arpeggiation of chords, most often of the quick, violinistic type,
was so standard an expressive device that it was rarely indicated at
all. That was probably due to the inadequacy of the symbol notation
available, there being no signs specifically for rapid breaking of
chords but only those that indicated a more leisurely succession of
tones, which was not always desired.

Ex. 35   Couperin's and Rameau's Arpeggiation Signs

Whether indicated by symbols or fully written-out, the basic forms of the ornaments used in harpsichord music can be grouped under six general headings: trill, mordent, appoggiatura, slide, turn and arpeggio.

THE TRILL

The trill, sometimes still referred to by its older English name of 'shake' is indicated by various signs, the most common of which are *tr* , *tr⸺*, +, ⫴ and ⫴ . It consists of an alternation of the main note, that over which the sign is placed, with the note either a semi-tone or a full tone above the main note, as the tonality may require.

Trills can be divided into two classes, long and short. Long trills very often—and especially when placed over dotted notes—end with a momentary dwelling on the main note (the French term for this, *point d'arrêt*, expresses the thought well) and possibly a termination in the form of a turn as well.

Ex. 36   J. S. Bach, Gigue, French Suite, No. 6 (BWV 817)

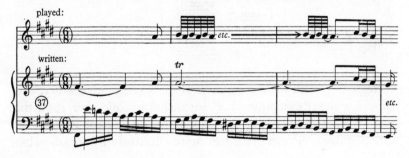

Ex. 37   *F. Couperin*, Les Folies Françoises: *1er Couplet, 13th Ordre*

In the earliest times, from the fourteenth to the sixteenth centuries, trills generally began with the main note.

Ex. 38   *Frescobaldi*, Toccata, *No. XI (Book II, 1637)*

Beginning with some composers of the seventeenth century, and almost without exception in all harpsichord music after 1650, the trill, whether short or long, started with the upper note. But even in earlier music, one can often trill more effectively by commencing on the upper note, which has the effect of giving the trill more harmonic 'bite' because of the appoggiatura effect of starting with a tone foreign to the harmony.

Ex. 39   Gibbons, Gagliardo *(Parthenia, No. 16)*

Ex. 40   Gaillarde (No. 3 of Attaignant's Quatorze Gaillardes *of 1531)*

In any doubtful situation it is well to work on the assumption that the trill should begin from above. If this should not prove feasible, simply because the requisite number of notes cannot be fitted into the available time-space, or if the musical effect is unfortunate (producing parallel fifths, for instance), then a trill beginning with the principal note can be considered—possibly with an initial holding of that tone. Alternatively, one might dwell for a moment on the upper note before starting the actual trill.

Ex. 41   Frescobaldi, Toccata, No. X *(Book II, 1637)*

A possible interpretation of Frescobaldi's irregular seven-note group.

Ex. 42   Handel, Courante, Suite, *No. 8*

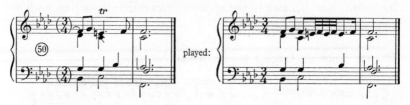

played:

In very quick progressions, a short appoggiatura or a turn can replace the trill.

Ex. 43   D. Scarlatti, Sonata, *K.20 (L.375)*

The short trills can be replaced by short appoggiaturas, even acciacaturas, if their *etc.* realization as [music] or [music] proves impractical at the required tempo.

Ex. 44   J. S. Bach, Finale, Sonata for Harpsichord and Viola da Gamba, *No. 2 (BWV 1028)*

The turn in bar 52 is probably the correct realization of the trill in bar 51.

The problem is less acute where composers have left us precise instructions. Couperin, for example, insists rigorously that all trills begin from above, and shows us two possible forms of such trills even where the preceding note is the same as the trill's upper one.

5. Harpsichord by Johann Adolph Hass, Hamburg, 1764
Russell Collection of Early Keyboard Instruments, Edinburgh

6. Harpsichord by Pascal Taskin, Paris, 1769

Russell Collection of Early Keyboard Instruments, Edinburgh

Ex. 45   F. Couperin, Table of Ornaments

Ex. 46   F. Couperin, Table of Ornaments

Other clavecinistes were less doctrinaire on this point but used a
special symbol to show trills beginning, exceptionally, on the main

Ex. 47   Dandrieu, Table of Ornaments

note. C.P.E. Bach follows Couperin, indicating (in company with
his German contemporaries) that where only

Ex. 48   C. P. E. Bach, Essay

is desired, it will be indicated as shown, in small notes, rather than
by use of a trill symbol, which for him means at least four notes in
the ornament.

9

Ex. 49   *C. P. E. Bach,* Essay

⑤ Halber oder
   Pralltriller

Where the upper note is indicated by an appoggiatura placed
before the principal note and the trill symbol, one should emphasise
or linger on the auxiliary before starting the trill.

Ex. 50   *J. S. Bach, Prelude, No. 4, W.T.C. I (BWV 849)*

Such appoggiaturas do not imply that trills which lack them should
start on the main note. In French music particularly, such an appoggiatura is frequently required even where it is not specifically
indicated.

Ex. 51   *F. Couperin, Rondeau,* Le Dodo, *13th Ordre*

(Even fewer beats may sound well.)

Ex. 52   *Rameau,* Musette en Rondeau

In the case of long trills, after an appropriate number of beats, one would end by dwelling momentarily on the main note. In the case of such a long trill over a dotted note, most often the trill would consume the value of the note minus its dot (more often a double dot in actual effect), leaving the *point d'arrêt* to fill out the value of the dot, as shown above in Ex. 37; or, on occasion, the *point d'arrêt* would be turned into a rest, a kind of emphasis by silence, and the trill brought to and end with a turn.

Ex. 53   *J. S. Bach, Prelude, No. 10, W.T.C. I (BWV 855)*

A termination of the long trill by means of a turn was also customary, unless, however, the note on to which the trill note resolved had already been anticipated.

Ex. 54   *Simple Cadential Trill*

Ex. 55   Cadential Trill with Anticipated Resolution

If the composer wished specifically to indicate the final turn, he could do so in a variety of ways:

Ex. 56   Signs for Trills with Turned Termination

Ex. 57

All three forms in Ex. 56 are played:

Usually the trill with a turn at the end will be played in a continuous manner as shown in the above examples. Occasionally, when the final turn has been written out in short note values, a *point d'arrêt* may be appropriate.

Ex. 58   J. S. Bach, Fugue, No. 13, W.T.C. II (BWV 882)

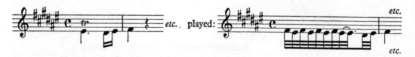

Sometimes prefixes to long trills were called for, either from below or from above.

Ex. 59   J. S. Bach, Andante (II), Italian Concerto (BWV 971)

Even more beats
can be played,
possibly with
acceleration from
a slow initial turn.

Ex. 60   J. S. Bach, Andante (II), Italian Concerto (BWV 971)

Again, more
beats with
acceleration
would be
appropriate
if played
with ease.

Ex. 61   Other Notation for Trills with Turned Prefix

To give particular emphasis to a cadential trill, it is quite in style
to add a prefix to an ordinary trill.

*Ex. 62   J. S. Bach, 1st Movement, Brandenburg Concerto, No. 5
(BWV 1050)*

One principal function of the trill, especially long ones which end in a turn or anticipate the note of resolution, is to give point to a cadence. This effect is familiar from the standard trill which ends so many cadenzas in classical concertos. Those cadenzas, as we know from their name, are really expanded cadences.

Another function, which concerns short trills most of all, is that of enlivening the musical line, brightening and high-lighting it, so as to give it a kind of gleam or shimmer. This kind of trill in its shorter form is characteristically used in a descending line.

Ex. 63   J. S. Bach, Italian Concerto, *No. 2 (BWV 971)*

Trills, like turns, can also be used to accent and point up notes reached by larger intervals.

Ex. 64   J. S. Bach, Fugue, No. 15, W.T.C. *I (BWV 860)*

There is also the basic sustaining function of the trill shown in a number of the preceding musical examples.

THE MORDENT

The mordent is indicated by the sign ⤳ placed over the note. Certain French composers, Louis (though not François) Couperin, Rameau and others, and occasionally Bach, too, used the sign placed after the note. Purcell and his contemporaries in England used the symbol ⤳ which in every other time and place denoted a trill, not a mordent. A mordent consists of the alternation of the main note with the tone either a semitone or a whole tone below, as the tonality requires. (See Ex. 26.) Thus, the mordent is the reverse of the trill. In later times, as with the trill, composers sometimes indicated any chromatic alteration of the lower note by a sharp or a flat placed below the mordent sign.

Ex. 65   *F. Couperin*, Les Folies Françoises: *1er Couplet, 13th Ordre*

Most but not all mordents are short, consisting of but a single alternation of main note and lower auxiliary. In its longer form, the mordent was sometimes indicated by a correspondingly longer sign ⤳ which, however, can be confused with signs for the trill with a turned ending. Couperin sometimes used a special term *pincé continu* for a long mordent.

See, for example, Couperin's *Musette de Taverni* in the 15th Ordre for an actual
pincé continu of comparable extent.

Ex. 66   F. Couperin, Table of Ornaments

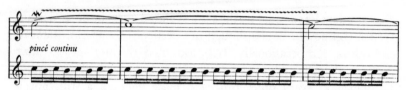

A mordent over a note of longer value may quite properly be
extended even though the sign used is that for the normal mordent.

Ex. 67   J. S. Bach, Italian Concerto, No. 2 (BWV 971)

(The mordent in bar 28 of the same movement can be even more extended)

Mordents never have any termination other than the filling out
of the remaining value of the main note after the mordent has been
played. But they can be introduced by an appoggiatura, particularly
in French music, Purcell and Bach.

Ex. 68   F. Couperin, Table of Ornaments

Ex. 69   *Rameau,* Gavotte

Ex. 70   *Purcell, Posthumous Table of Ornaments*

Ex. 71   *J. S. Bach, Sarabande,* French Suite, *No. 5 (BWV 816)*

The functions of the mordent are linked to its basically dissonant character. Its name suggests the bite it should have. Most often it is used to decorate rising musical lines or those using repeated notes, as well as to accentuate leaps that imply or outline the harmonic pattern.

Ex. 72   J. S. Bach, *Gavotte I*, English Suite, *No. 3 (BWV 808)*

Ex. 73   F. Couperin, Le Carillon de Cythère, *14th Ordre*

Agréablement, sans lenteur

Ex. 74   F. Couperin, 'Le Croc-en-Jambe', *22nd Ordre*

Gaiëment

As in the case of trills, the number of repercussions and their speed must be decided in each instance by the musical effect desired. On especially resonant instruments in acoustically 'live' surroundings, fewer repercussions will be needed. On instruments having a sharp attack but less after-resonance or located in particularly 'dead' acoustics, more repercussions will be needed to produce the equivalent effect. It is always better to attempt fewer repercussions and time them with precision than give the listener the uncomfortable feeling that the performer is straining his technical powers to breaking point. While mordents are almost always performed rather quickly, trills vary in speed and can even accelerate from a slow start.

Ex. 75   J. S. Bach, Sarabande, Partita, No. 1 (BWV 825)

the trill gradually accelerates to *point d'arrêt*

etc.

THE APPOGGIATURA

The appoggiatura can be divided, like the trill and the mordent, into long and short categories. The long appoggiatura is always played on the beat. The short appoggiatura must often be played on the beat, too, but on many occasions will anticipate it, especially if that is necessary to avoid forbidden parallel fifths or octaves.

Ex. 76   J. S. Bach, (a) Variation 13, Goldberg Variations (BWV 988)

The short appoggiatura must be played before the beat to avoid the ugly parallel octaves between B and C.

etc.

Ex. 76 continued overleaf.

Ex. 76 continued   *(b) Sarabande,* Partita, *No. 6 (BWV 830)*

The appoggiatura must be played before the beat to avoid ugly parallel fifths:
A–E, B–F sharp.

An appoggiatura, generally speaking, is any adjacent accessory
note, i.e. not more than one degree of the scale away from the note
it decorates. Its function is to fill out and connect intervals greater
than a second, and give an expressive sighing effect if played long,
or a kind of snap if played short.

In fact, many appoggiaturas are written out in ordinary notation.
Others are written in smaller characters, presumably because such
appoggiaturas were originally in contravention of some rule of
strict counterpoint or possibly sufficiently at odds with the figured-
bass line to represent impermissible dissonances. The forbidden
dissonance was shown by the use of smaller notes in somewhat the
way in which forbidden words were printed with dashes replacing
some or all of their letters.

Ex. 77   Handel, 3rd Movement, Suite, *No. 2*

etc.

Composers did not trouble as a rule to write the smaller forms of
note used for appoggiaturas in the correct note values. That might
have been too explicit, too close to the forbidden dissonance!
Instead they used an arbitrary or conventional value, generally a
quaver, and left it to the performer's good sense and musicality to
achieve the correct value.

Instead of the smaller form of note, some composers used a special
sign for the appoggiatura.

Ex. 78   Special Appoggiatura Symbols

Used by many *clavecinistes*, including Rameau, and occasionally by J. S. Bach.

Ex. 79   Special Appoggiatura Symbols

Henry Purcell (posth.) 1696

Ex. 80   Special Appoggiatura Symbols

Chambonnières 1670

As a crude 'rule of thumb' for playing long appoggiaturas—the ones which lean on the following note with a kind of sighing effect—the following is offered, particularly for first readings of pieces:

An appoggiatura takes half the value of the main note which follows it, except that if the main note is dotted, the appoggiatura takes two-thirds of the value.

Ex. 81   Appoggiaturas: Typical Patterns

Ex. 82   Appoggiaturas to Dotted Notes

In certain contexts, usually in $\frac{6}{4}$ or $\frac{6}{8}$ metre, appoggiaturas before a pair of tied main notes will often take the entire value of the first of that pair.

Ex. 83   J. S. Bach, Prelude, No. 19, W.T.C. II (BWV 888)

This appoggiatura could also be imitated in the bass part at the third beat of bar 19 at the performer's option.

In a somewhat similar way, an appoggiatura can also take the entire value of the main note, which is then sounded in the time of the written rest. The most famous instance of this occurs in the E flat major prelude from Book II of Bach's *Forty-Eight*:

Ex. 84   J. S. Bach, Prelude, No. 7, W.T.C. II (BWV 867)

In working out the proper values for appoggiaturas we must keep the dissonance function clearly in mind. If too long a value softens the dissonance too much, then try and shorten the appoggiatura. The collision of the main note with another note in a different voice so as to form a unison or open octave should similarly be avoided. In sum, finding the best resolution of appoggiaturas is a matter of determining the correct quantity of dissonance to spice the music.

Short appoggiaturas, while written in the same small notes as the long ones so as to be superficially indistinguishable from them, usually sound best when played quite short, and slightly before the beat. Certain of the old authorities mention the short appoggiatura but the background material is admittedly rather sketchy. Short appoggiaturas are in any case relatively rare in classical harpsichord music. Here are two examples of Scarlatti's use of what seem to be short appoggiaturas.

Ex. 85   D. Scarlatti, Sonata, *K.133 (L.282)*

Ex. 86   D. Scarlatti, Sonata, *K.216 (L.273)*

Very often an appoggiatura which merely repeats the preceding note or notes of the line will sound best when played quite short.

Ex. 87   J. S. Bach, Variation 13, Goldberg Variations, *(BWV 988)*

In other contexts, particularly in slower pieces, a longer repeated-note sighing effect is called for and the appoggiatura should be extended in length and played on the beat.

Ex. 88   J. S. Bach, Variation 25, Goldberg Variations *(BWV 988)*
The second endings only of each section of the variation are shown, but both first and second are the same in all material respects.

The shortest form of appoggiatura is also known by another Italian name, acciaccatura, literally 'squashed note'. The true acciaccatura is played virtually simultaneously and on the beat.

7. Harpsichord by Burkat Shudi and John Broadwood, London, 1782
Victoria and Albert Museum, London

8. Harpsichord by William Dowd, Boston, Massachusetts, 1963

(*Photograph by George M. Cushing, Boston*)

Basically it is a kind of mordent rather than an appoggiatura. These are either notated in the usual appoggiatura fashion,

Ex. 89   F. J. Haydn, 1st Movement, Sonata, *Hoboken XVI,37*

or shown as simultaneous dissonances that look like twentieth-century note-clusters in the manner of Ives and Bartok.

Ex. 90   J. S. Bach, Scherzo, Partita, *No. 3 (BWV 827)*

But short appoggiaturas and acciaccaturas were never written ♪ before the nineteenth century to distinguish them from longer ones in the ordinary smaller note form ♪. Any such distinction between short and long appoggiaturas found in modern editions of harpsichord music is purely editorial, not original.

The rational choice amongst the possible alternatives will largely depend on one's feeling for and tolerance of dissonance. But purely rhythmical considerations also play a part in fixing the most appropriate length. In doubtful cases there is little one can do except try the alternatives, one by one, and make the best choice one can.

During the eighteenth century—though never before—we occasionally find small notes which appear to be appoggiaturas in form but which are, in fact, intended as connecting notes. These are played rather short and take their value not from the main notes that follow them, but from those that precede them.

Ex. 91   *Quantz*, Essay

The Germans had a special name for this kind of passing note, *Nachschläge*, literally 'after-beats'. They were usually intended to fill in a pattern of main notes outlining a triad. Thus, in Bach's *B* major prelude from the second book of the *Forty-Eight*, we might play the passage in this fashion, although ordinary appoggiaturas could also serve.

Ex. 92   J. S. Bach, Prelude, No. 23, W.T.C. II (BWV 892)

François Couperin uses these 'after-beats' occasionally but, alone among the major harpsichord composers, he indicates this in his table of ornaments by slurring them to the preceding rather than to the following note.

Ex. 93   F. Couperin, Table of Ornaments

To sum up, there is no substitute for taste and experience if you wish to play appoggiaturas correctly and convincingly. The possibilities of long or short, or perhaps something in between, must be weighed as well as the related question as to whether an appoggiatura is better performed accented on the beat or unaccented before the beat. On the harpsichord with its very limited capacity for dynamic nuances, the effect of some of these shadings and degrees of accent can only be created by two complementary means: the timing of the appoggiatura and following note, and the degree of overlap between them. As we have seen, a kind of diminuendo can be produced by a complete overlap, releasing the first long appoggiatura note only after the second has been sounded.

THE SLIDE

The slide, often known by its German name, *Schleifer*, or its French one, *coulé*, sounds just as its name implies. It is usually indicated by symbols:

Ex. 94   *Chambonnières, Table of Ornaments*

coulé

Ex. 95   *F. Couperin, Table of Ornaments*

tierce coulée,   tierce coulée,
en montant   en descendant

Ex. 96   *D'Anglebert, Table of Ornaments*

coulé sur   autre
une tierce

Ex. 97   *J. S. Bach, Gavotte II,* French Overture *(BWV 831)*

Ex. 98   *Purcell, Table of Ornaments*

but occasionally it is written out in small notes or in normal notation.

Ex. 99   *Quantz,* Essay

Ex. 100   *J. S. Bach, Aria,* Goldberg Variations *(BWV 988)*

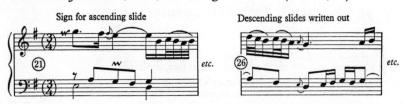

If a longer slide or *tirata*, as it was known in Italian, is required, it will almost always be written out in small notes; otherwise it will take the form of a straight line between the outer notes of the figure. Note, however, that the straight line used by François Couperin between note-heads is a sign of legato and does not signify a slide or any other ornament.

Ex. 101   F. Couperin, Le Trophée, 22nd Ordre

Ex. 102   D'Anglebert, Table of Ornaments

Ex. 103   F. Couperin, La Morinète, 8th Ordre

As one assumes with all ornaments, the three-note slide is most often played on the beat and only occasionally before it. Longer slides have to be interpreted in their contexts and they are, in any event, rather infrequent.

THE TURN

The turn is indicated by the sign ∾, which is occasionally placed vertically 𝆗. The timing of its execution will vary with the tempo.

Ex. 104   C. P. E. Bach, Essay

When placed between two notes, the execution is different.

Ex. 105   Turn between Notes   Ex. 106   Turn after a Dotted Note

Inverted turns were rare before 1750. They were indicated thus:

Ex. 107   C. P. E. Bach, Essay, Inverted Turn

Purcell and his school were once again idiosyncratic in their symbol notation. The turn sign was placed over the note, but the turn was intended to sound as if the symbol had been placed between two notes.

Ex. 108   Purcell, Table of Ornaments

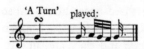

A puzzling ornament occurs frequently in the works of François Couperin, though less often in other music. It was long thought that it should be realised almost like an ordinary trill with a turned termination. But some scholars maintain that it is a turn plus a trill without any termination, instead:

Ex. 109   Purcell, Table of Ornaments

Couperin does not give any interpretation in his otherwise very complete table of ornaments. But he normally indicates trills with turned terminations in the ways common to other composers. Possibly, as has been suggested, this symbol was to direct us to make a substantial pause between the opening beats and the turned termination, but the contexts in which it was often employed do not always permit this.

Ex. 110   F. Couperin, Passacaille, *8th Ordre*

The turn has a number of functions, dependent on tempo and note values. It can serve simply as a grace to connect elements of a conjunct line, usually a rising one. A turn can set off the final note of phrase. Less biting and dissonant than the mordent, it can still serve to provide accentuation and relieve monotony in slower tempi by decorating a line of repeated notes. In quick tempi the turn will often be useful as a substitute for a full trill, especially where a cadence is approached by a wide interval.

THE ARPEGGIO

The arpeggio, or breaking of chords, is more than a mere ornament, it is a vital part of harpsichord technique. It is very rare that a chord is struck as a solid block of tone. For one thing, on a correctly regulated multi-register instrument, the different sets of jacks will not pluck exactly at the same instant but will do so in a predetermined staggered order. This is necessary for technical reasons for, if all the jacks plucked at the same time, the touch would be much harder.

(Some modern German instruments, nevertheless, are normally so regulated as to produce simultaneous plucking. The touch on such instruments is certainly very different from any historical models known to the writer—and these include some German ones.)

But even on a single register, subtle arpeggiation of virtually every double note and chord is really an integral element of sensitive harpsichord playing. Chords can often seem richer and fuller when broken ever so slightly, and so much so as to be beyond the average listener's threshold of perception. But the student should not neglect to learn how to strike a chord with absolute precision and simultaneity of plucking, for there are many occasions where that kind of firm sound is musically appropriate. In no sense should arpeggiation become a mere mannerism, as it did in the playing of certain late nineteenth-century pianists.

A whole spectrum of arpeggiation possibilities can be observed by the attentive player. It ranges from the slow, expressive, often dream-like succession of the single notes of a chord to the sharp, abrupt, forcefully accented playing of a chord which is scarcely broken—like the sound of a violin playing a triple- or quadruple-stop as loudly and as swiftly as it can. The combinations of arpeggios upwards and downwards at varying rates of speed, with interpolated or repeated notes, and with figurations, are almost limitless in their potential variety.

An important use of arpeggios was realising figured-bass parts in a manner at once rich and uncluttered, and adding rhythmical interest to progressions of chords of an often conventional, almost banal pattern. The arpeggiations of many Bach preludes, including the *C* major from Book I and the *C* sharp major from Book II of the *Forty-Eight*, for instance, are perfect examples of how arpeggiation was used to vary and colour the fundamental harmonies. In these preludes, of course, the patterns used were scarcely of the unimaginative, jejune type frequently encountered in the works of lesser masters.

The French school developed certain refinements of notation beyond the usual vertical wavy line | for arpeggiation. This sign is still in use today, though it now invariably indicates an upward break. The direction of arpeggiation could be shown thus:

Ex. 111   *F. Couperin, Table of Ornaments*

Ex. 112   *Rameau, Table of Ornaments*

Ex. 113   *Chambonnières, Table of Ornaments*

Additional non-harmonic notes, broken chords combined with acciaccaturas, could also be shown in their more precise notation:

Ex. 114   *D'Anglebert, Table of Ornaments*

Ex. 115   *Rameau, Table of Ornaments*

Ex. 116   F. Couperin, Passacaille, *8th Ordre*

Rameau's form of notation for arpeggiations with added notes between the chord intervals was used by Bach, amongst others.

Ex. 117   J. S. Bach, Sarabande, Partita, *No. 6 (BWV 830)*

This chord can also be played slightly arpeggiated.

The combination of arpeggios and such inserted notes foreign to the actual chord, like cloves spicing the music, was a decorative technique used to vary reprises. Bach's own example illustrates this perfectly:

Ex. 118   J. S. Bach, Sarabande, English Suite, *No. 3 (BWV 808)*

The indication *arpeggio* applied to a group of block chords is a direction to play them from the bass up to the treble and down again, sometimes more than merely once, as we see in examples from Handel and Bach:

Ex. 119   Handel, Prelude, Suite, *No. 5*

(*Ex. 120* overleaf)

After surveying the principal categories of keyboard ornaments, we will now have some notion of their musical functions and their proper realisations. But how does one deal in practice with actual pieces of music? In the first instance one must determine whether the composer himself has left us any directions. Among the great 'five' of the eighteenth century, for instance, we can thank Couperin and Rameau for quite comprehensive directions. Handel and Scarlatti, however, left us nothing. Bach falls into a middle category. His table of ornaments in the *Clavierbüchlein* for his son Wilhelm Friedemann follows d'Anglebert's table for his pieces published in 1689. But Bach's table does not begin to cover all the symbols that he used in his music. Still, the available evidence seems to put Bach in the French camp, at least in the absence of compelling musical reasons to realise particular symbols used by him in accordance with the practice of other schools.

Ex. 120   J. S. Bach, Chromatic Fantasy *(BWV 903)*

played (according to a contemporary manuscript):

As a practical matter, most harpsichordists seem to take French eighteenth-century practice, that of Couperin and Rameau, as their working basis—their operating hypothesis, their system of presumptions—for playing all music of the late seventeenth and eighteenth centuries. Even for much of the earlier literature such an approach is usually quite practical. Where it does not achieve convincing results, as in the case of Frescobaldi or certain works of Froberger, then musical sense and the experience that comes with trying various alternative solutions will guide us to a rational solution. The amount of solid objective data about how most composers ornamented their music is too slight for us to pretend that anything but pragmatically derived solutions to many problems can be attempted. In a word, we are and are likely to remain disappointingly ignorant.

The virginalists pose a special problem. Besides writing out in full many of their more complex formulas of ornamentation, notably cadential trills, they and their copyists often liberally sprinkled single and double slanting strokes through the note stems. To this day no one has succeeded in assigning precise meanings to these signs. What is more, in some virginal books they are absent. In others, including many important ones and among them *Parthenia*, the sole contemporary publication, they are very much in evidence. In different copies of the same piece they are hopelessly inconsistent.

Here again, taste and experience must guide us. Nimble fingers on responsive keyboards sounding instruments with a crisp, sharp tone can indulge themselves to the limit and play practically all the ornaments suggested by these strokes. Less agile hands, more ponderous actions, especially resonant instruments—these militate against playing any but a few, well-placed ornaments in virginal music. The suggestion often made that single strokes should be interpreted as slides or appoggiaturas, and double strokes as mordents, short trills or appoggiaturas, does not prove of much practical help. For one thing, there are frequently just too many single strokes; such a plethora of slides and appoggiaturas make a musical muddle. Mordents and little trills generally come off best, the former when the line rises and the latter when it falls. Needless to add, any edition of virginal music replete with modern symbols for trills, mordents and appoggiaturas has been edited very subjectively and should only be used with great caution if at all.

The subject of free ornamentation, the improvised addition of decorative elements not indicated by the composer, is one which deserves intense study on the part of any harpsichordist. A detailed discussion of the subject would fill many chapters, but it would still not offer any more authoritative guidance. By its nature improvisation defies systematising. It is doubtless wise to work from those few, highly important examples of written-out ornamentation

which have come down to us: the *doubles* of the French school and
Bach's *English Suites*, the variant versions of many of Bach's pieces
in the manuscript copies made by his various pupils, and those few
recorded versions of what must originally have been improvisations,
such as Handel's chaconne in G major with sixty-two variations.
Contemporary transcriptions for harpsichord of operatic music, like
Babell's of Handel and d'Anglebert's of Lully, tell us much about the
great freedom enjoyed by performers and how it was exercised.

At the start, it would be well to limit one's efforts to the filling-in
of the more obvious lacunae. For instance, many cadential trills
were conventionally omitted as it was expected that they would be
supplied automatically by the performer.

Ex. 121   J. S. Bach, 1st Movement, Brandenburg Concerto, *No. 5*
    (BWV 1050)

Other omissions of ornaments would result from the practice of
only indicating them with the appropriate symbol at their first
appearance, after which they were to be provided by the player.
Such is often the case in fugues, where the subject is routinely given
its trills or mordents only the first time round, as we have seen.
Arpeggiation is also frequently shown only partially in this manner,
not merely by harpsichord composers; Liszt often showed it for no
more than the first few of a series of broken chords.

In the earlier stages it will be wise to write out free ornamentation of, say, the repeat of a dance movement from a suite. Later on it may be wiser to refrain from committing too much to paper, for ideally each performance should offer new, improvisatory elements.

We are still only on the threshold of rediscovering in full what was first perceived by pioneers like Arnold Dolmetsch more than half a century ago: that throughout the whole history of Western music from Perotinus to Verdi, free ornamentation was applied to a far greater extent than it usually is today in the playing of such music. We, who are concerned with the music of so many styles and epochs, naturally bear a far heavier burden in this regard than did the older musicians who only played the music of their contemporaries. We can begin to acquit ourselves of this obligation to the composers of the past if, modestly, discreetly and with all the taste our inexperience allows, we begin to touch in a detail here and there. Doing more than this in a manner both tasteful and convincing demands years of study and experience.

XI

UNEQUAL NOTES AND OTHER
RHYTHMICAL ALTERATIONS

No aspect of the performance of older music is more fraught with controversy and less characterised by consensus than this vexed topic. Scholars dispute, critics quibble, and performers despair. What is the neophyte, the inexperienced, the tyro to make of it all?

There is no avoiding any element which is part of the task of performance. We cannot ignore even those that can be dealt with only tentatively. In the present chapter we are concerned with three conventions which in our time might be considered the unfortunate results of imprecise notation but which in earlier days were accepted without much of a quibble, hence the dearth of substantial information about them until well into the eighteenth century. But the origins of these three practices go back far earlier than the time of Couperin or that of Quantz and C.P.E. Bach—even further than Frescobaldi.

The first of these, and the most difficult to understand in theory and to apply in practice, was the conventional playing of certain notes, written as equal in value, in ways which redistributed their length and stress as if they had been notated as unequal. It was long thought that this practice was mainly confined to French music and to a very few other composers of different national schools, such as Frescobaldi, who had prescribed it more or less specifically. There is now a growing mass of evidence to justify the belief that unequal notes were used far more widely than this, though considerable scholarly controversy still rages over the temporal and geographical extent of their use.

There seems little doubt that the second type of rhythmical alteration—variable dotting (mainly over-dotting so as to truncate the following note or upbeat group)—was widely practised throughout the period we are concerned with by all national schools. The third type—the assimilation of duple note values to a prevailing triplet rhythm—persisted much longer, only dying out in the late nineteenth century.

UNEQUAL NOTES

Whether the old scale-fingering of two- and three-note groupings, partially avoiding the use of the thumb and the little finger, led to unequal notes, or whether these fingerings were themselves in part the result of such inequalities of rhythm, is a moot question. Unequal notes were not entirely limited to keyboard music. Be that all as it may, the fact is that *unequal notes are appropriate in conjunct movement*, in other words in scale-like patterns where each note moves up or down one degree of the scale from the preceding and to the following note. The inequality involved relates to each pair of such conjunct notes, i.e. is *an articulation by twos*. The more usual pattern is a long-short pairing, what the French termed *lourer*.

Ex. 122   Rameau, Musette en Rondeau

The less common pattern is the short-long pairing, called *couler* by the French, and indicated either by a simple slur over pairs of notes or by a slur plus a dot over the second of the pair.

Ex. 123   Purcell, A New Ground (*Ƶ.T682*)

Ex. 124   F. Couperin, Les Moissonneurs, 6th Ordre

The note values to be played as unequal are usually (but not always) the half-beats, that is, those corresponding to half of the denominator of the time signature fraction. For example, a piece in $\frac{3}{4}$ would have unequal quavers (eighths), one in $\frac{3}{2}$ unequal crotchets (quarters), and so on.

In the case of the long-short pairing pattern, the more common of the two, we have only negative indications to guide us. Thus, long-short pairs should not be used where:

1. Short-long pairs are indicated by two-note slurs with or without a dot between the second note-head and the slur, as just explained; or
2. There is an express command to play equal notes.

Such express commands forbidding inequality include:

1. Words such as 'notes égales', 'également', 'vite', 'vif', 'marqué', 'mouvement détaché', 'décidé' and the like;

Ex. 125   *Rameau*, Les Niais de Sologne

Ex. 126   *F. Couperin*, Les Folies Françoises, *13th Ordre*

The time signature ½ as well as the strange archaic notation in white crotchets (not quavers) are reproduced from the original edition.

7e couplet—La Langueur

Ex. 127   *F. Couperin*, Le Turbulent, *18th Ordre*

2. Symbols showing that the notes are not to be paired: dots (which do not mean staccato, incidentally), dashes, and wedges (which can mean staccato or merely an accent placed over or under the note-heads); slurs over more than two notes;

Ex. 128   *F. Couperin*, Le Carillon de Cythère, *14th Ordre*

3. An Italian indication, such as 'andante', in French music.

There are other implied reasons for playing equal notes:

1. Intervening rests or shorter note values, which in any event break up the pairing of the notes;

Ex. 129   Dandrieu, Les Tendres Reproches *(Book II)*

2. Syncopations;

Ex. 130   F. Couperin, Les Baricades Mistérieuses, *6th Ordre*

3. Repeated notes, which belie the conjunct scale type of line anyway;

Ex. 131   Dandrieu, Le Caquet

4. A very fast or vigorous tempo, even if not indicated by a word such as 'vite' or 'presto'.

Ex. 132   Rameau, Rondeau, Les Cyclopes

If the line of unequal notes begins with a rest, then that rest is treated as if it were the first of an unequal pair of notes.

Ex. 133   F. Couperin, La Favorite, *3rd Ordre*

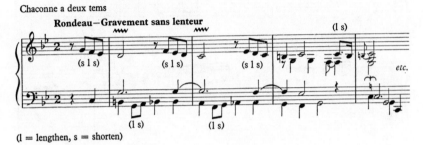

(l = lengthen, s = shorten)

The note values usually affected are the half-beats, those equivalent to half the value of the denominator of the time signature, as already explained; thus, for instance, in $\frac{3}{1}$ minims (half notes), in $\frac{3}{2}$ crotchets (quarter notes), in $\frac{3}{4}$ quavers (eighth notes), in $\frac{3}{8}$ semiquavers (sixteenths) and in $\frac{3}{16}$ demisemiquavers (thirty-seconds). However, it is not always so simple and clear. Where the signature is simply 2 or 3 without any denominator, then quavers (eighth notes) are to be played unequally. Where the signature is 4 or its equivalent C, or $\frac{3}{4}$, semiquavers (sixteenths) are the unequal values. ₵ is ambiguous because it was often mistakenly used to indicate four quick beats rather than two in a measure. If the ₵ is really played 'in two', then the quavers (eighths) are unequal, but if 'in four' the semiquavers (sixteenths) are. Another seeming exception is $\frac{2}{4}$, which most of the time is played 'in four' (i.e. as $\frac{4}{8}$) rather than 'in two', so that it is the semiquavers (sixteenths) which are unequal.

Both the old authorities and the modern scholars are divided in their opinions on a further complexity: should not only the note-values specified as unequal above but also all smaller note values in the particular metre be played unequally? Experience suggests that this should probably be done only on rare occasions. Too much inequality merely engenders aural confusion.

Ex. 134   Jacquet de la Guerre, Sarabande

But here again taste and musical sense must guide us, not so-called 'rules'.

Allemandes were a special case, according to the writers on the subject of unequal notes, though, of course, their lines do not usually proceed in pairs of notes. Thus, they were most often but not always to be played with equal notes. Where an exception to this rule was to be made, the composer would sometimes so indicate.

Ex. 135   F. Couperin, Allemande, La Laborieuse, *2nd Ordre*

★**Sans lenteur; et les double croches un tant soit peu pointées.**

★Not slowly; the semiquavers slightly dotted.

Occasionally a slight dwelling on the first of a four-note group, a kind of 'long-short-short-short' but very subtle, is effective and was even recommended by a few of the old authorities.

Inequality affects the top part in the main and does not apply to inner voices except where consistency requires it.

Ex. 136   F. Couperin, *Chaconne*, La Favorite, 3rd Ordre

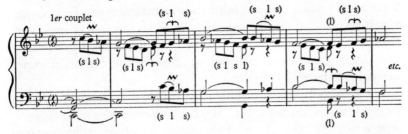

Now, what is meant by 'long' and 'short'? Long-short pairs can be made up of a normal length first note followed by an abbreviated second one; however, that is really more a type of articulation than an actual redistribution of note-lengths. The reverse is true of short-long pairs. Such articulations are certainly part of what is involved and in many instances may suffice altogether to give the requisite impression of inequality. But the actual duration of each note of the pair must be considered in the light of the prevailing mood and tempo of the piece, too.

In a faster, livelier context a more abrupt, snappier rhythm is called for than in a slower, more gentle one. The contemporary writers give us little specific information on this question of relative duration. Some modern ones have suggested varying arithmetical solutions, dividing two notes in a 3:1 or a 1:3 ratio, the equivalent of, say, a dotted quaver followed by a semiquaver, or vice-versa, respectively. Those ratios are perfectly conceivable as proper at times. But the range of possibilities is surely much broader and, accordingly, less susceptible to reduction to absolute and precise numerical values. The ideal distribution of durations and relative weights in each case must be worked out from the material of each piece, taking proper account of its mood, tempo, pattern of prevailing note values and rhythms.

Finally, in what music are we to use the unequal note convention? In French works unquestionably, for it was the French who codified the system and wrote about it. In the case of Italian music, it would seem that we should apply inequality in the case of the earlier composers such as Merulo, the two Gabrielis, Frescobaldi and possibly Michelangelo Rossi (i.e. composers who wrote before

1650), possibly limiting our use of unequal notes to works in the toccata and prelude cast and other freer forms and types. Frescobaldi is quite explicit on the point in reference to his toccatas, as we know from the directions for their proper performance in his 1637 publication. Many dances, too, can take on additional lilt and life if some inequality is tastefully applied.

In the case of the virginalists the situation is uncluttered by any factual information whatever. The few authentic virginalist fingerings which we have, allow of the possibility of inequality, indeed almost make it unavoidable, but experience suggests that equal notes, carefully articulated in short groups, are what is really called for by this music. By the time of Purcell, however, unequal notes seem to have been commonly played, doubtless owing to the French influence which came with the Restoration. So, in the case of English music, one might well apply the opposite of the 'rule' for Italian works: that is, one could play occasional English works after 1650 until about the time of Handel with inequality but not earlier music of the virginalist school.

There is considerable evidence that inequality was widely employed in the music of the older Spanish school centring round Cabezón. But there seems to be none at all in respect of later periods, such as eighteenth-century music of the Padre Antonio Soler type. Domenico Scarlatti, whether he is considered as Italian or Spanish for this purpose, should only be played with equal notes.

German music, the product of Europe's most eclectic cultural environment, should be dealt with in the light of the above conclusions. If, for example, we are dealing with an unquestionably Italianate work, say one of Kuhnau's sonatas, inequality would seem inappropriate. But if the piece in question were one of Kuhnau's suites, very much in the French style, then unequal notes might be called for and should be tried experimentally. In the case of such Francophiles as Georg Muffat, senior, a Lully disciple, and J. K. F. Fischer, to whose suites the French style of performance is much more clearly appropriate, the presumption in favour of unequal notes is correspondingly greater.

Such of Bach's music as is strongly under French influence, the suites most especially, can often benefit from inequality in the

Gallic tradition. This is a point of view that can be supported both on historical grounds and on musical ones. Many scholars oppose doing so, despite evidence of the practice found in many German sources close to Bach's time. Certainly there are many isolated slurs over groups of more than two notes in Bach's music that can be most satisfactorily explained as directions to play equal notes rather than indications of 'legato' or 'phrasing', as editors have usually sought to do. Obviously inequality has no place in Bach's fugues or other polyphonic works in the tradition of the great German organists. If the player decides to attempt the use of unequal notes in Bach's music, he should begin with the French-style dances: the courantes (not the Italian corrente-type with fast semiquaver patterns), the sarabandes, the passepieds, the bourrées, certain minuets (especially those entitled 'menuet' rather than the Italian or German form of the word) and the like. But it does not do to appear doctrinaire on a subject which is still under examination.

Handel is a less difficult case. Most of his music strikes one as far more Italianate than French, certainly in comparison with Bach's. Even the dances of the suites are much closer to the Italian form in virtually every case. As a general rule unequal notes should, therefore, be avoided in playing him.

Almost no harpsichord music appeared after the middle of the eighteenth century, although very late clavecinistes like Duphly still brought out an occasional book of pieces after that date. Our consideration of unequal notes ceases at this point. But it should not be thought that unequal notes did not flourish later on or have not been used, to a certain extent, in other periods. Any sceptic can easily verify this statement by analysis of recordings of dance pieces. Much of the lilt of Schubert *Ländler* and the rubato of Chopin mazurkas in actual performance derives from just such inequality as we have been discussing: not the rigid kind involving precise arithmetical ratios but one involving far more subtle distinctions. This is so even though the pianoforte, with its dynamic shadings, does not need to rely to the same extent as the harpsichord on differentiations of timing. Like so much else that is 'rediscovered' from time to time, we find in the end that unequal notes have never really been lost!

VARIABLE DOTTING

The use of more than a single dot to indicate the prolongation of a note may have begun earlier than 1756 when Leopold Mozart claimed credit for inventing this in his violin method. But for many years afterwards, and even in the music of Leopold's son, many single-dotted notes continued to be played on occasion as if double-dotted. In fact, to this day one often hears a military band play a march written in ordinary dotted rhythm as it if were a double-dotted one.

Earlier composers were no more consistent in their use of dotted notation. Complications arose, for instance, from the French tradition of unequal notes. How did a French composer show that a dotted quaver, say, followed by a semiquaver should be played so that the first note was decidedly longer than the first (long) note of an unequal part? He sometimes added a word like 'pointé' or 'piqué' to stress the distinction. More often he added nothing, leaving it to the player to use his common sense and musical feeling to guide him to the conclusion that very often dotted notes should be longer when played than in the notation.

But it was not only in the French tradition of unequal notes that over-dotting was employed. Italian and German composers used it frequently, too. Therefore, any dotted rhythm should always be examined closely to see whether possibly some over-dotting closer

Ex. 137   *Dandrieu, Ouverture, La Lully (1st Suite, 1728)*

to the 7:1 ratio of double-dotting rather than the 3:1 ratio of single-dotting may not be in order.

As a rule in simple metre dotted notes do not exist in isolation save in those few instances where longer notes plus dots are used to fill out an entire bar, or part of one, at the end of a section or of an entire piece. Ordinarily, dotted notes are followed by shorter ones written in a value one-third as long as the preceding dotted note, or by a group of shorter notes serving as an upbeat to the next element of the musical line, especially in the familiar French overture pattern.

Ex. 138   J. S. Bach, French Overture *(BWV 831)*

As shown in the interpretations in the musical examples, these were adjusted in performance to sound as if they were written in double-dotted notation or an even more extreme rhythmically contrasted form. The dotted note was extended in duration and the following short note or upbeat group drastically shortened accordingly.

This was not a practice limited solely to French music by any means. Bach's C minor partita, for example, begins with a Sinfonia in the Italian tripartite form which opens with a dotted rhythm, written and played as shown below.

Ex. 139   J. S. Bach, Sinfonia, Partita, *No. 2 (BWV 826)*

Observe from the interpretation in the above example that if the first note of a dotted group comes after a rest, and this note and the preceding rest are both written in equal undotted values, one should lengthen the rest and shorten that first note to accord with the prevailing rhythm. This procedure is analogous to the practice when playing unequal notes in such a context, as we saw in Couperin's *La Favorite,* Ex. 133 above. A helpful mnemonic in both cases is *tarantara* in Gilbert and Sullivan's *Pirates of Penzance!*

In slower contexts more can be done by way of over-dotting than in faster ones, where the distinction necessarily becomes less clear-cut. Here are some further examples from Bach and Scarlatti to show how variable dotting can be applied both in slow and fast tempi.

Ex. 140   *J. S. Bach,* Toccata *(BWV 912)*

Ex. 141   *J. S. Bach,* Sarabande, French Suite, *No. 5 (BWV 816)*

Ex. 142   *J. S. Bach, Variation 26,* Goldberg Variations *(BWV 988)*

Ex. 143   *D. Scarlatti,* Sonata, *K.238 (L.27)*

At cadences, where a trill is added to a dotted note before the resolution, double-dotting will also result quasi-automatically in faster tempos, since if played strictly as written, there would hardly be time for the trill at all.

Ex. 144   J. S. Bach, 1st Movement, Brandenburg Concerto, *No. 5 (BWV 1050)*

But even in slower tempi such an extension of the trilled tone is usually called for, if only to allow for an adequate *point d'arrêt*—a sufficient holding of the note after the beating of the trill before it resolves.

Ex. 145   J. S. Bach, Sarabande, English Suite, *No. 6 (BWV 811)*

A related notational problem arises where, instead of using a dot, the composer employs tied notes to achieve the same effect. It is interesting, in this connexion, to compare Bach's notation of the opening bars of his *French Overture* in the earlier version in C minor with that in the familiar, later B minor version first printed in the second part of his *Clavierübung*.

Ex. 146   J. S. Bach, French Overture (C minor version)

Ex. 147   J. S. Bach, French Overture (BWV 831)

Very often, especially in French music, upbeat groups after a rest or a tie linking them to a preceding long note ought to be shortened as shown in the following example.

Ex. 148 *Chambonnières*, Sarabande Grave (*No. 75*)

ASSIMILATION TO TRIPLET RHYTHMS

Although triplet notation showing that three notes are to be played in the time normally taken by only two notes of the same value can be traced back to the fourteenth century, it is only quite recently —since the time of Brahms in fact—that it has been used uniformly and precisely. Bach, for example, wrote the last movement of his fifth *Brandenburg Concerto* in one manner while setting down the gigue of the *A minor English Suite* in another.

Ex. 149 *J. S. Bach, 3rd Movement*, Brandenburg Concerto, *No. 5* (*BWV 1050*)

Ex. 150   J. S. Bach, Gigue, English Suite, *No. 2 (BWV 807)*

The placing of the semiquavers in the autograph of the concerto
shows clearly that Bach intended the same musical result as in the
gigue, a $\frac{6}{8}$ metre with a prevailing triplet rhythm.

That is one kind of triplet problem. Another is presented by two
notes in one voice set against a triplet in the other. This can occur
with two equal notes, or with two notes in a dotted pattern.

Ex. 151   Rameau, Les Niais de Sologne

Ex. 152   J. S. Bach, Courante, Partita *No. 1 (BWV 825)*

As to the simple duplet, the evidence seems fairly clear that it
was performed as if the first of the two apparently equal notes were
twice as long as the second, exactly as shown in the interpretation
given in Ex. 151. There is, however, a slight conflict of authority
between two of the principal codifiers of performance practice in
the mid-eighteenth century—Quantz and C. P. E. Bach. They
appear to differ, at least on paper, as to whether the second note of

the dotted pair coincides with the third note of the triplet or comes after it (i.e. being played in exact conformity with the notation). While recognising that on occasion the after-beating effect of literal performance may be more striking—Mme. Landowska played the courante in Ex. 152 thus with great verve— usually the assimilation of the dotted pair of notes to the prevailing triplet rhythm is to be preferred, not only for Ex. 152 but in other similar pieces.

Ex. 153   *J. S. Bach,* Courante, *French Suite No. 4 (BWV 815)*

There are many other troublesome passages and pieces of this type, particularly in Bach's music. The *E* minor fugue in Book II of the *Forty-Eight* is really quite simple to decipher:

Ex. 154   *J. S. Bach,* Fugue, *No. 10, W.T.C. II (BWV 879)*

but how does one deal with the *D* major prelude in the same volume?

Ex. 155   J. S. Bach, Prelude, No. 5, W.T.C. II (BWV 874)

Many other examples of notation apparently at odds with a triplet rhythm could be shown and elucidated. A genuine poly-rhythm of two beats against three, or three against four, will be mandatory in the rare situation where both parts are thematic and thus cannot be rhythmically altered without being distorted. But the generally applicable principle of assimilating all such seemingly inconsistent notes and note-groups to the prevailing triplets should be clear enough from the examples already cited, for it easily to be applied in all analogous cases.

XII

REGISTRATION

For the beginner at the harpsichord, the temptation to try out the entire palette of available tonal colours is irresistible. It is certainly of some practical value to become acquainted with your instrument in this way. But, once this normal curiosity has been gratified, it is time seriously to consider the proper use of these timbres in the artistic performance of music.

Ideally every harpsichordist should be required to commence his studies on an instrument with only one 8-foot stop. I say this not because I believe in a colourless, grey treatment of the music, but rather, because it is only by learning to exploit to the full all the other expressive resources of the harpsichord that you can prepare to use registration to greatest effect. An obvious analogy here would be with the graphic arts, with the relationship between drawing and painting. The ability to suggest hue and shade by the use of a monochromatic line—the landscape drawings of Rembrandt come particularly to mind—has been developed to the highest degree by the greatest of painters.

Even if your present instrument offers only a single 8-foot stop, and even if you never play on any more complex instrument, the principles expounded in this chapter are nonetheless of vital importance. After long study, when registrations suggest themselves automatically from the very look of the printed page, it is still enormously revealing to play many a piece through a few times on that single basic register.

Obviously one cannot discuss registration in twentieth-century music for harpsichord since, for better or for worse, contemporary composers almost invariably prescribe their own. All too often excessively detailed indications of registration changes are given, based on limited experience with particular instruments. The earliest generation of modern harpsichordists, some of whom continued to perform well into the age of the long-playing gramophone record, are now seen to have depended too much on registration, and even to have done violence to the music at times by too frequent changes of tone-colour. There are still well-known artists whose playing is as much an exercise in registration pedal virtuosity as it is in manual dexterity.

To a considerable extent this over-registration can be explained by the characteristics of the instrument employed. As we noted in the discussion of the revival of the harpsichord, many types of instrument developed in those earlier stages of the revival—those often still heard in concerts and on records—were constructed on false premises. It was thought that by the use of heavier construction, often with an iron plate as in the modern piano, and thicker strings at higher tensions, a larger and fuller tone would result that would be adequate to the concert halls of our time. It has been demonstrated that, in fact, the perfected instruments of the seventeenth and eighteenth centuries, and modern instruments similarly constructed, are not only louder in terms of decibels and of carrying power, but also their individual registers are both tonally purer and much more agreeable to the ear. The excessively tense strings of the pianoforte type of harpsichord produce a harsh tone and, because of the force and heavy plectra required to pluck them, exclude the possibility of true legato playing. The harpsichordist using such an instrument has no choice but to change the tonal colours as frequently as possible in the hope that a variety of less beautiful sounds may prove acceptable substitutes for a pure and lovely tone.

The earlier generation of modern players were still under the spell of certain nineteenth-century notions, notably the belief that not merely had mankind and technology evolved in a steady progression towards perfection but the same tendency was also to be observed in matters of art. It was often remarked that if Bach had known the modern type of instrument he would have been only too pleased to have his music performed on it. This point of view of course overlooks the fact that the harpsichord, like the organ and even the violin of Bach's time, was a perfected instrument. If he had composed for the harpsichord of 1912 or the pianos and organs of that time, he would have written quite different music for them. Finally, the late nineteenth-century musical aesthetic was one which placed greater emphasis on colour than on line. One has only to think of the lush orchestration of the works of Strauss, the Russian school and the French impressionists to appreciate the environment in which the pioneers of the modern harpsichord revival were trying to re-establish their instrument.

The addition or subtraction of registers on a harpsichord does not produce anything like as great an effect in either a dynamic or a colour sense as is commonly believed. Therefore, except where colour contrasts are heightened by the music itself—through shifts of tessitura, drastic thickening or thinning of textures, and all manner of rhythmical and harmonic devices—the actual stop or combination of stops employed at a given moment only provides a basic coloration. The ground of the picture is determined by this, but the detailed shadings, the fine tones, the subtleties of line, are created by the player through nuances of touch. Too frequent changes of registration will tend to obscure or fragment the form of a piece without necessarily lending it tonal variety.

Let us now consider the tonal possibilities of the various registers. Given the wide range of variation amongst modern instruments, it is still practical to make certain generalisations. The first of these is that the back 8-foot or lower manual 8-foot is thought of as the basic harpsichord tone, equivalent in this sense to the 8-foot open diàpason of the organ. It is the standard by which all the other stops on the instrument will be judged by the listener. Opposed to it is the front 8-foot or upper manual 8-foot which is more nasal in tone because of the difference in plucking points, as previously explained. In a two-manual instrument these stops will be of about equal volume. On a one-manual instrument the front 8-foot will usually be voiced slightly more softly.

The two 8-foot registers alone offer an enormous range of tonal possibilities. Indeed, as we know from òur consideration of the development of the classic instrument and the music written for it, they suffice to perform the great majority of works written for harpsichord. The combination of registers in a good instrument has a synergistic effect, the whole being apparently greater than the sum of its parts. The compound sound seems fuller and more forceful than one might expect, probably because of certain disharmonies which result from the plucking of two sets of strings: it is more than the mere addition of one to the other. A genuine tutti effect on the harpsichord is best obtained by the blending of two such 8-foot registers.

The 4-foot register not only strengthens the volume of the sound but also lends a sharper edge, a highlight to the tone, somewhat the way mixture stops do on the organ. By a curious acoustical phenomenon, the 4-foot adds profundity to a solid 8-foot bass tone in a good instrument.

In addition to its use in combinations, the 4-foot stop on many harpsichords may be used as a soft solo register—one also somewhat nasally coloured. Where the compass permits, a 4-foot solo stop will often substitute effectively for a missing 8-foot lute register (the optional second register on the upper manual of a double harpsichord which plucks very close to the nut). Echo effects an octave higher than written were often contemplated even in the keyboard music of the sixteenth century for, as we know, little ottavina instruments were sometimes set on top of ordinary virginals for this purpose. The 4-foot will sometimes serve on a two-manual instrument to outline a highly florid cantilena (played an octave lower than written, of course) but the accompaniment must be carefully toned down to permit this. That is necessary because the 4-foot must always be voiced quite a bit softer than either of the 8-foot stops if it is not to dominate the tutti, making it shrill and rasping, or perhaps suggestive of an octave transposition.

On two-manual instruments with the 4-foot on the upper keyboard—a disposition only now gradually disappearing from the Central European scene after fifty years of unjustified dominance—the tutti use of the 4-foot in such instruments is rather more difficult to work out. While the most basic tutti sound is that of the two registers of 8-foot pitch combined, the addition of the 4-foot to the back-plucked lower 8-foot is of far wider application than its combination with the upper 8-foot. As an example of the problem created by this displacement of the 4-foot register to the upper manual, consider the usual registration on a resonant instrument of concerto-grosso type movements such as the preludes of Bach's *English Suites*. One would oppose a tutti of 8-foot and 4-foot, or even both 8-foot plus 4-foot on the lower manual to a solo of upper 8-foot—or as an alternative the combination of two 8-foot registers as the tutti. Only the second alternative will be available on the Central European type of harpsichord. Using the upper manual 8-foot plus 4-foot would give too nasal and unsubstantial a tutti sound, while the lower 8-foot used against it would likely sound too full for effective contrast. It would be rather like the use of massed flutes and oboes to contrast with the string section of an orchestra, an effect that would be far from what was intended. Unless one had three feet, it would be impossible to pedal one's way out of this dilemma. And even that unusual advantage would not help in passages requiring one hand to play the tutti and the other the solo. The normal complement of feet will suffice on such harpsichords, however, to pedal out the 4-foot when a contrasting piano tone on the upper manual, a single 8-foot, is required.

While the tutti quality of the upper 8-foot and 4-foot combination is markedly inferior to that of the lower 8-foot plus 4-foot, it is still highly useful. Bright but unsubstantial, it lends itself to gay dances or carillon pieces rather than to the tutti sections of works written in imitation of the concerto grosso.

The use of contrasting 8-foot stops on the two manuals is another type of registration that is more useful than might appear from its infrequent prescription in the classical repertoire, where it is limited to a few *pièces croisées* and the dialogues in certain of the *Goldberg Variations*. The lute stop on the upper manual plucking close to the nut will find application as a solo stop rather more often than as an ingredient of a combination or tutti, although the exotic sound of lute stop and 16-foot appeals strongly to some ears.

The *peau de buffle* register optionally available on the lower manual as a second 8-foot stop can be used most effectively as an accompaniment and, to a lesser extent, in combination. It is an ideal soft accompaniment to the upper 8-foot. Admittedly unhistorical because the introduction of the *peau de buffle* dates from a period after 1750, the register is nevertheless of great utility in playing the classical harpsichord repertoire, carp as the scholars may. The most useful combination of *peau de buffle* with another register is its blending with the 4-foot. This has a special dark quality with a rich, full sound which belies the relatively small volume it produces. The combination in fact replaces in considerable measure the beguiling tones of a 16-foot and 4-foot combination, producing, apparently, for acoustical reasons, something of the same 'hole in the middle' of the sound as if there were a spread of two octaves rather than only one between the stops.

Finally, we turn to the 16-foot stop, a very controversial register which enjoys less popularity today than it did earlier on in the harpsichord revival. As we have already seen, this is a register which must be counted as a rarity historically: it is certainly not one which was considered standard on the large two-manual instrument, even at the peak of its flowering in the eighteenth century. If its occasional addition—mainly to German instruments—did not lead to its widespread general acceptance as an enrichment of the instrument's capacities, we can only assume that the composers of the time, who were also its leading virtuosi, did not insist on it.

Certain combinations, such as a blend of 4-foot and 16-foot, even lute stop and 16-foot, can sound very beautiful, especially in slow movements. The stop can occasionally be used in a solo capacity, usually an octave higher than written to cancel out the octave transposition, or as an accompaniment stop softly contrasted with the upper manual 8-foot.

But considerations of historical authenticity aside, the inclusion of a 16-foot stop often has adverse effects on the tone quality, as we have seen, particularly in the bass section of the 8-foot registers. Thus, there is a constant temptation to add the 16-foot to compensate for the weakness of the bass line. Unfortunately, except in slower tempos, the effect is to muddy the sound and, in extreme cases, produce veritable tonal cannon shots. Therefore it is a register to be used with discretion and caution, and it should be voiced as softly as possible. Applied with restraint and taste, the 16-foot stop can be of great effect. It might be used this way only a few times during an entire recital. Used indiscriminately in complex polyphonic textures or in fast moving music, it will create a jumbled confusion.

Buff or harp stops are usually provided on even the smallest and least complex instruments. On large instruments they are usually fitted to either the lower or the upper manual 8-foot stops and, on many modern German harpsichords, to the 16-foot as well. In single harpsichords the buff stop is often so arranged that it can be applied to either the lower or the upper segments of the keyboard, or to both, as some of the early Flemish makers often did. This 'split buff' points up the principal use of the stop as an accompaniment, particularly where there is an arpeggiated figuration in slower tempo in the manner of a lute accompaniment. For example, in playing sixteenth-century lute dances, optionally performable on keyboard instruments even at that time, a buff stop can be used effectively in repeating a section previously heard on a normal register. A buffed register can rarely be combined effectively with any other.

Unless a softly leathered *peau de buffle* register is available, the distinction between leathered and quill plectra for registration purposes will not usually be exploitable on a single instrument. The use of quill for one 8-foot register and normal hard leather for the other frequently creates problems of tonal incompatibility. Generally a maker will opt for a leathered type of instrument or a quilled one.

Half-hitch pedals or piano hand-stops, in addition to their effect on their individual registers, also have a marked effect on combinations. The full harpsichord at half-hitch can often yield a very different sound from the same registration at full-hitch. Certain combinations of half-hitch registers are sometimes very effective; the 4-foot and upper 8-foot combined at half-hitch can be ravishingly beautiful in pieces such as Couperin's *Le Carillon de Cythère* and the G major prelude from the second book of the *Forty-Eight*.

The full tutti sound, normally two 8-foot and one 4-foot registers combined, has a tonal value which in the best instruments will seem to exceed the sum of its parts. The addition of a 16-foot stop to the tutti will add an organ-like solidity on the infrequent occasions when it can be used without sacrificing tonal clarity.

The extent to which the full tutti is employed will vary in direct proportion to the resonant quality of each instrument. On the best of harpsichords the occasions for its use will be fewer; on the worst, even the employment of all registers simultaneously will not yield the desired richness and plenitude of sound. No simple formula will be enough here. One can only suggest that, following our basic principle of under- rather than over-registration in doubtful cases, the player should reserve the *plenum* for climactic moments wherever possible. To cite one example, in Bach's *French Overture*, which lasts almost half an hour, the full tutti will not be heard except in the opening movement, the overture proper, and the final Echo movement where it is used in opposition to the piano level of the upper manual. In the *Goldberg Variations*, which go on far longer, its use is only called for by the music in Variation 16, again a French overture, and possibly in Variation 30. Too frequent use of the full power of the instrument will reduce its power to make a climax where one is really called for.

Having now considered the qualities of individual registers and their various combinations, we pass to the real task before us: registration of the music that we play. Let us first of all review the historical evidence regarding harpsichord registration. (Historical organ registrations are not really to the point, and attempts to make analogies from them to the harpsichord have yielded nothing of value.) There are occasional indications of forte and piano in Bach, Rameau and others as well as a few titles or markings ('a 2 clav.', or opposed forte and piano dynamic levels) specifically prescribing a two-manual instrument. That is all the direct evidence we possess except that the *pièces croisées* and other late French pieces give express directions for registration to produce imitations of instruments or bird songs. The few early harpsichord methods are surprisingly silent on the subject.

There are no doubt many reasons for this dearth of guidance. For one thing, much of the finest harpsichord music was not published but was only played by the composer and his immediate circle of pupils. Thus the registrations to be employed either for whole categories of pieces or for particular ones would have been known to those who would be playing them. Another important reason was that the available instruments varied widely even within one period and style. Single and double virginals co-existed in Elizabethan and Jacobean England. Spinets and single-manual harpsichords of varying degrees of complexity were found in Italy in all periods. So were they in the Netherlands and Flanders before and after the development—presumably by the great Antwerp builders —of the expressive two-manual instrument. All manner of harpsichords were used in Germany where the clavichord was also more frequently encountered than elsewhere. In the case of published music, too, the composers and publishers did not wish to restrict the potential use and sale of the printed scores too much. If anything, they usually presented the music that was printed as suitable for all kinds of keyboard instruments. Of course, in parts II and IV of his *Clavierübung* that call for double harpsichord Bach had no choice but to indicate that fact clearly in the titles. Couperin, on the other hand, was careful to offer alternative means of performing his *pièces croisées* on a single manual and even on non-keyboard instruments.

Thus we see that very little mandatory registration from the composers' hands has come down to us. With rare exceptions we are free to do as we please—or to do as best we can. How, artistically or even ethically speaking, are we to proceed? For one thing, we can reflect on the development of the historical instrument, considering the type of harpsichord for which composers presumably wrote. From this we can at least learn what we should avoid in the way of registrations. Certainly William Byrd did not conceive of a piece such as 'The Bells' in the Fitzwilliam Book as one to be played with an artificial gradual crescendo, beginning on the softest register and adding stops progressively, including the 16-foot— Heaven help us!—until the deafening conclusion is finally reached. Byrd, who did not dispose of such tonal resources, had instead to write his dynamic scheme into the music which he did with a master's hand.

But must we go to the other extreme, limiting ourselves rigorously to those means that we know with certainty were available to the composer in question? To do so in our age—when playing older music for ears which have heard *Tristan* and *The Rite of Spring*—may be to cloak it in too drab a tonal garb. But if one admits of a need to liberalise the canons, how far should this freedom extend? Would it justify the hypothetical over-registration of the Byrd piece just discussed?

Initially and ultimately, this question must be settled by the good taste of the performer, the court of first and last resort in this instance. To our ears and sensibilities, the essential point is that registration, like all elements in a convincing interpretation, must appear to the listener as organic, deriving directly from the musical structure, and must not be grafted or superimposed upon it. (Changes of registration, whether by pedals or hand-stops, must obviously be effected without awkward pauses or stumbling from a technical point of view.)

In arriving at a registration, we must ask ourselves questions such as: does a particular section or movement call for a simple sound, i.e. the sound of a single register; or for two opposed single registers; or for compound sounds, i.e. those of combined registers, possibly opposed to those of a single register? In the case of shorter movements, especially those in a suite of dances, the question will be more easily answered. With a suite or other multi-movement work, variety of colour will also necessarily be a factor. But what is one to do with a longer movement in concerto style or, most important of all, with a fugue?

Making due allowance for acoustic factors—performance in the drawing room or the concert hall—and the nature of the piece, we can draw analogies from the instrumental or, still better, the orchestral music of the same or a related style. A French overture movement will surely call for the massed complex of sounds of a full orchestra, even with trumpets and drums in the case of pieces in *D* major or *C* major, traditionally used with those instruments. On the other hand, the trio of a minuet can be conceived of as a treble line of oboes against a bass provided by bassoons. In more abstract works, particularly toccatas and other sectional forms, we must decide which are the full, heavy-sounding portions and which ought to be lighter in tone.

In fugal works a similar rule-of-thumb might be established for playing the exposition, the counter-exposition, stretti and coda, say, at a higher dynamic level, and the intervening episodes at a lower one. Unfortunately, fugues often seem to be a seamless web and resist dissection into neat, concerto grosso-type alternating sections. Well as such an approach may succeed on the pianoforte or the clavichord, it is often impracticable on the harpsichord. Frequently one settles with regret for a very restricted range of dynamic and colour changes, only to find to one's delight and surprise, that they have been written into the music itself.

There is an unfortunate tradition in romantic organ playing which still is prevalent, that of beginning a fugue as softly as possible and gradually adding stops until the end is played with every one of them engaged. Schweitzer decried this procedure more than sixty years ago and urged that the first statement of the fugue subject should be made in a clear but not overpowering forte. The playing of fugues by the best modern organists on antique organs or modern 'baroque' instruments has demonstrated the essential correctness of the classical approach and does suggest that in the playing of fugues on the harpsichord registration changes should be limited in a similar way to those clearly required by the structure of each fugue.

In general one tends to avoid the use of octave doublings with 4-foot or 16-foot until the very end of a fugue. Such octave stops, it is often said, have a tendency to confuse the part-writing in the ears of the listener. Actually the 4-foot can frequently be used in combination without muddying the fugal texture in the least; indeed, it can clarify it. The 16-foot stop, on the other hand, can only properly come into play in a coda, as a rule, just as some organists throw in a pedal reed stop at the end of a long and powerful organ fugue.

But rules of thumb can serve as nothing more than that. The essential task in fugue playing remains to understand the musical structure so thoroughly that the entire interpretation, including registration, grows organically out of the form of the work. One does not need to have studied counterpoint in all its complex theoretical ramifications in order to understand how a fugue is put together. It is enough to have determined how each of its parts relates to the others, regardless of whether one is familiar with the technical terms for the parts or the relationships. There is no reason for a person of musical sensitivity to be frightened by technical jargon, or his ignorance of it.

Pauses in the course of the music, relatively short ones included, suggest the possibility of a change of registration even on hand-stop instruments. Whenever they occur, they should be viewed from that aspect. While a relatively long pause may be required for coupling or uncoupling keyboards by pushing or pulling one of them in or out, a short pause even on the part of one hand often suffices to withdraw or add a register. In fact, one may sometimes lengthen a brief pause for other valid musical reasons and incidentally add or subtract a register. For example, in the penultimate measure of the Sinfonia of Bach's partita in *C* minor, one can quite easily

Ex. 156   J. S. Bach, Sinfonia, Partita, *No. 2 (BWV 826)*

use the little breath of a pause after the first dotted note to add another register. Stylistically it would be quite in order to lengthen the dot in this case to cover the extension of the following rest before attacking the ensuing shortened semiquaver and playing the following cadential trill and chords.

If each of us possessed a collection of harpsichords on which we could match the music to the instrument, the case for rigid adherence to individual historical precedent would be far stronger, though still not iron-clad. That great and noble species of the breed, the English harpsichord of the eighteenth century, for example, was not identified closely with a particular repertoire specially composed for it, save for the works of such latter-day minor figures as Roseingrave and Arne. When Anna Magdalena Bach copied Couperin's *Les Bergeries* rather freely into her *Clavierbüchlein* of 1725, she surely did not do so in anticipation of playing the piece on a French instrument imported into Saxony for the purpose. And in general, not only was music composed and published for harpsichords in their widest sense, but we often cannot say what sort of an instrument some very important composers like Froberger, for instance, intended as the vehicle for realising it.

However, even if we are not so strictly bound by history as has been pretended, that fact nevertheless confers no blanket licence to include all sorts of anachronistic effects such as quasi-crescendi and diminuendi by the addition or subtraction of pedalled registers, the chopping of music into tiny bits, each with its own registration, and the indiscriminate use of special colorations in all manner of pieces. The truth lies between these extremes.

Yet there is only so much that can be imparted by the written word. Each harpsichordist, each acoustical environment, each instrument and each work interact in ways which cannot be considered in the abstract. Summarising the conclusions expressed in this chapter, or restating them in other words, would not add to the reader's preparation for his task. For all its importance, registration is but one of a number of means at the disposal of the harpsichordist for bringing the music he plays to life. By itself registration will not suffice. Conversely, even in the total absence of registration changes, much beautiful music can still be made on the simplest of instruments.

XIII

ENSEMBLE PLAYING

Throughout the entire original flowering of the harpsichord, it served as an indispensable element in almost every ensemble used in secular music. It provided keyboard accompaniments for the entire range of concerted works from solo sonatas to operas and cantatas. This tradition persisted from late Renaissance times through the Baroque age down to the threshold of the nineteenth century. Haydn, for example, still conducted his London symphonies in the 1790s from the keyboard. The ubiquitous keyboardist was indeed the busiest of all musicians for more than three centuries.

Yet, strange to tell, few of the literally thousands of harpsichord parts of the period which have survived show anything more than a figured-bass line. From this shorthand notation, consisting of only the bottom part of the music supplemented more or less fully by numerals and accidentals to indicate the harmonies, the harpsichordists of the day improvised realisations that performed the essential functions of an accompaniment: to assert and to reinforce the rhythmical flow of the music, and to provide the harmonic, and even some contrapuntal, filling-out of the texture: to support the ensemble in the fullest sense.

Thus, vital elements in the performance of ensemble music were left to chance. Likely as not some realisations fell far short of perfection when played by less skilled musicians. But the entire training of keyboardists was founded on the thorough-bass, the system of keyboard harmony worked out from a figured line. Amateurs as well were expected to work out their parts from a figured bass, and it was only after about 1840 that editions of old Italian violin sonatas, vocal music and Bach's chamber works, for example, began to appear with written-out accompaniments—most of them, alas, added by the editor in a contemporary style often quite at odds with that of the original.

While hardly any realisations of the period have come down to us, we are fortunate in having a wealth of didactic material to guide us. It is because thorough-bass was the framework on which the education of musicians, keyboard players most of all, was erected. For example, C. P. E. Bach's famous *Essay on the True Art of Playing Keyboard Instruments* devotes about half its length to figured-bass playing.

The art of realising keyboard parts from a figured-bass line has begun to be cultivated once more. A number of present-day harpsichordists and organists do it superbly. More often, however, the realisations one hears in the concert hall or on recordings can either be termed pedestrian, lifeless and stodgy, or else over-elaborate, fussy and precious. The complete union of capacity and taste is rare. Much more than a mere technical facility in translating notes and numbers into sounds is required.

But one must begin at the beginning. Some knowledge of harmony is indispensable at the start. Ultimately, of course, one will want to know the original source materials such as the Bach *Essay*. But they are not recommended as basic texts for the modern reader although they were designed as such originally. It is best to start by working through a simple harmony text and then turn to a handbook on the specifics of accompaniment from a figured-bass such as Hermann Keller's *Thoroughbass Method*, an excellent practical treatise.

Meanwhile, pending completion of this highly recommended home study course, there is no reason to abstain from ensemble playing. Whether it involves accompanying a friend's efforts on the recorder or playing a continuo in large-scale works, there will probably be some sort of written-out keyboard part available. The quality of such pre-packaged merchandise varies widely. That is necessarily the case because no printed part can take account of the different instruments and circumstances of performance which affect the realisation. Some will be harmonically 'correct' but utterly devoid of rhythmical life and instrumental colour. Where older realisations are used, especially, one will encounter elaborate 'piano accompaniments' in a completely nineteenth-century idiom, so thickly written as to be virtually unplayable in any event on the harpsichord which has no damper pedal to bridge the chasms between the chords. The solution to this problem is to be daring and as tasteful as the circumstances permit.

The 'hymnal' type of accompaniment in four parts moving in block formation can be vastly improved straight off by breaking up the clumpish chords into some simple figurations, using an occasional ornament to decorate the simple line. The lush, romantic, overblown type of accompaniment is more difficult to deal with. Here we must simplify drastically.

First of all, make sure what the bass line really is. They scarcely ever descended below *C*, the lowest note of the violoncello, although octave doublings using lower notes were and should be used at climactic points. Thinning out the chords, possibly breaking up the rhythm into shorter values, or, alternatively, reducing the frequency of the chords in the right hand and similar rhythmical devices will often help enormously.

Experiment by all means and do not hesitate to 'fake' the style of the composer, to imitate it in every way you can. Such an effort is neither meretricious nor presumptuous; on the contrary, it goes to the essence of the figured-bass player's task. If you have a highly-edited text, you may find that a library possesses a scholarly edition of the work without unstylistic accretions from later hands. Comparison of the two texts will at least enable you to verify what the printed harmonies add to, or subtract from, the original figured-bass part. Many arrangers of realisations have not hesitated to substitute more complex, more 'interesting' harmonies for the simpler progressions of the original figured-bass.

We have only a few old keyboard parts written out in full. They were probably those which had to be realised in full because the composer wished to incorporate independent contrapuntal lines or thematic material into the keyboard parts. Hardly any consist of the kind of rhythmically activated chord progressions and figured harmonic skeletons that form the basis of thorough-bass realisations. Since the works which do have written-out keyboard parts are important parts of the repertoire, it would be as well to make their acquaintance earlier rather than later. But they are not easy to play in themselves, ensemble considerations apart. For example, Bach's sonata for harpsichord and flute in B minor (BWV 1030) boasts a richly elaborated keyboard part. Nothing needs to be added by the performer here except an occasional ornament for consistency's sake. The entire slow movement, Largo e Dolce, can be taken as a model of the simple but highly effective style one can employ to accompany from a figured-bass such a florid cantilena as the flute part in this movement.

An intimate acquaintance with all the Bach sonatas possessing full harpsichord parts will certainly stand one in good stead. For the most part, the six sonatas with violin (BWV 1014-1019) are written in three independent lines, one for the fiddle and two for the harpsichord, almost like trio sonatas for organ. Occasional slow movements, however, do have keyboard parts resembling what might have been a figured-bass, though most modest talents will not be up to imitating Bach's example so effectively when faced with an actual figured part.

The three sonatas for harpsichord and viola da gamba (BWV 1027-1029) will most often have to be performed—if at all—with viola or violoncello until viola da gamba players become more plentiful. Portions of the keyboard part are written as figured bass lines in the latter two. It is strange that having written out the keyboard part almost completely, Bach did not write out these few bars .in full, too. Again the texture is almost exclusively trilinear with virtually no purely harmonic functions assigned to the harpsichord except in those few figured-bass measures.

Of Handel's keyboard writing in chamber music we really have only one example, a modest sonata in C major for *cembalo concertato* and viola da gamba. The second slow movement of this affords some insight into what Handel's realisations may have been like but there is more to be learnt from a close examination of his solo harpsichord music, so clearly derived from figured-bass practice. See, for example, the chaconne in G major with its sixty-two variations on an eight-bar ground bass. Note the many changes Handel was able to ring on that simple harmonic progression. Not all the figurations will be directly applicable to the accompaniment of chamber works but many will.

One of Bach's pupils, Kirnberger, provided a realisation of the third movement of the trio sonata from his master's *Musical Offering* (BWV 1079) and the other three movements were similarly treated, albeit less skilfully, by an anonymous eighteenth-century musician. Even this less than inspired keyboard part can be studied with profit; most of us would be happy to be able to do as well. The sonata is quite daring harmonically for its time and extremely difficult to play at sight, which is probably why the part had to be written out. (It is reprinted in Hans David's edition of the *Musical Offering* published by Schirmer.)

Another later example of a first-class realisation was provided by none other than Brahms who wrote out the accompaniments very stylishly indeed for six of Handel's duets (Ed. Peters 2070). The original basses were not even figured, as was often the case, which makes Brahms's achievement all the greater.

The French have left us nothing to serve as a guide to realising their figured-basses except theoretical writings. The harpsichord parts in Rameau's *Pièces de Clavecin en Concert* are far too much in the style of solo keyboard music to be considered as models for realisations.

The playing of ensemble music is a subject which lends itself less to the written word than the performance of the solo repertoire. The fundamental difficulty in playing chamber music with the harpsichord is usually dynamic balance, which in turn depends on the number and types of the other participants. Almost any harpsichord, the tiniest spinet included, can manage to accompany a solo instrument, though a recorder more easily, say, than a cello. But the mightiest double can rarely hold its own against the forte of an orchestra unless the latter plays with great discretion. In figured-bass playing, it was normal practice, and still is, for another instrument, usually a viola da gamba or violoncello, or sometimes a bassoon, to double the bass line in chamber music. In the orchestra, of course, all of these, variously doubled in turn, joined in reinforcing the bass line.

The doubling of the bass part is very helpful in sustaining longer notes which the harpsichord cannot. But problems of coordination between the instruments do arise unless proper care is taken to articulate and phrase the bass part with due regard for the limitations imposed by length of bow or the need to take breath. Having the doubling instrument there can liberate the harpsichordist, too. He can pay more attention to the harmonic and rhythmical aspects of his role. For one thing, he need not repeat every one of those pounding repeated bass notes which sound well enough on the gamba or cello.

Ex. 157 J. S. Bach, 1st Movement, Trio Sonata, Musical Offering (BWV 1079)

The improvisatory nature and rhythmical functions of the keyboard part in ensemble music can hardly be stressed too strongly. Therein lies the secret of effective accompaniment just as much as in the correct realisation of the bass. Even when playing from a written-out part one should try to vary the realisation at each playing, working in an ornament here or a little bit of figuration there, as if improvising on the figured-bass.

But in the performance of a fully written-out obbligato harpsichord part, as in the Bach sonatas or the Rameau pieces mentioned above, the essential difference from a figured-bass lies in the similarity of musical materials allotted to each performer, especially the thematic imitations which occur both in the keyboard part and the lines played by the strings and wind. These often come in close juxtaposition, and unless the players coordinate most carefully, each will expose the others' limitations mercilessly. Many articulations and phrasings that are completely convincing on the violin, for instance, may be quite impractical from the point of view of the harpsichord.

In works of the linear type, such as the Bach sonatas for harpsichord obbligato and violin, flute or gamba, the three or four parts must function as equals, rather like the parts in a fugue. This is much more difficult to achieve than a satisfactory balance between a solo instrument, or two, playing with a harpsichord performing a figured-bass part with the bass line doubled by another instrument. In the latter case there is much more latitude as regards the upper lines of the keyboard part and the harmonies of the realisation. The listener can sense a harmony or a rhythmical pattern at a dynamic level much lower than that necessary for perceiving the details of a melodic line that relates contrapuntally to the other lines of the texture.

While mention has been made of dynamics, particularly as they relate to the balance between the instruments, it is clearly impossible to offer specific suggestions for registration in chamber music. This has to be worked out in performance. Little contemporary information has come down to us concerning what registrations were used in ensemble music. A few rare piano and forte markings suggest the use of a two-manual instrument though a single harpsichord can deal perfectly well with these if it has knee levers or pedals for changing stops. An assistant or page-turner who can manipulate hand stops in case of need is neither inartistic nor unhistorical, as every organist can confirm. In the case of figured basses realised on a very simple instrument without any means of changing registration, the only dynamic resource we have is to adjust the texture as required both in respect of thickness (number of parts) and rhythmical activity. By reducing a four-part texture to three, the harmony can be preserved while reducing the dynamic level slightly. By increasing the number of notes sounded consecutively or simultaneously, and by rolling the chords, even repeatedly at times, one can coax a great deal of sound out of a single 8-foot stop.

Fortunately there is much repertoire solo sonata and chamber music using the harpsichord as a continuo instrument that is technically simple and musically within the grasp of almost every player. The harpsichordist can learn a great deal from making music with players whose instruments are so essentially different from his. They will envy him the capacity of delineating lines so clearly. He in turn, will covet their ability to make dynamic nuances. For all the seeming inflexibility of the harpsichord, the sensitive performer will be able to keep pace with his ensemble partners provided he believes in his power to create an illusion of what they are actually able to produce on their instruments. A magician must first of all believe in the power of his magic. The competition and stimulation of ensemble playing make it an indispensable part in every harpsichordist's training in the artistic manipulation of his conjuring box of plucked wires.

XIV

THE HARPSICHORDIST'S LIBRARY

The principal purpose of the present book will have been largely achieved if it stimulates the reader to seek to know more about the harpsichord and the music written for it. We offer the following list of books in English which deal more fully with the facts and problems discussed in the preceding chapters, and finally some guidance in the matter of building a music library.

The basic work on the historical instrument is and will probably long remain Raymond Russell's *The Harpsichord and Clavichord: An Introductory Study* (London, 1959). The enthusiast who wishes to know even more about the construction of the historical instrument will find Frank Hubbard's *Three Centuries of Harpsichord Making* (Cambridge, Massachusetts, 1965) a virtually complete compendium of all available information about the materials and methods of the great instrument builders of the past.

An excellent summary of basic tuning and maintenance procedures is contained in Frank Hubbard's pamphlet, *Harpsichord Regulating and Repairing* (Boston, Massachusetts, 1963), basically intended for the use of piano tuners, but entirely comprehensible for the serious layman.

The music of the harpsichord in its classical period is adequately dealt with in chapters 2-5 of F. E. Kirby's *A Short History of Keyboard Music* (New York and London, 1966), which contains a very full bibliography. More scholarly works treating keyboard music in a fuller historical context are Gustave Reese's *Music in the Renaissance* (New York and London, 1954, rev. ed. 1959), and Manfred F. Bukofzer's *Music in the Baroque Era* (New York, 1947; London 1948).

Biographies of individual composers will be found most helpful where harpsichord music constituted the bulk of the particular composer's output. At the head of the list of biographies of the great 'five' of the eighteenth century one would certainly place Ralph Kirkpatrick's *Domenico Scarlatti* (Princeton and London, 1953), which is not only the definitive study of the man and his music but also affords insight into the musical thought and practical working methods of the author, a great harpsichordist as well as a scholar of the highest rank.

Wilfred Mellers' *François Couperin and the French Classical Tradition* (London, 1950; New York, 1951) serves as a guide through both Couperin's harpsichord music and the works of his predecessors and successors. Karl Geiringer's brief biography *Johann Sebastian Bach— The Culmination of an Era* (London and New York, 1966) takes account of recent fundamental changes in the accepted chronology of Bach's works.

Cuthbert Girdlestone's *Jean-Philippe Rameau: His Life and Work* (London, 1957) includes a full discussion of the keyboard music in chapter 2, one which is fundamentally sound in spite of the author's eccentric statement 'that Rameau's harpsichord music gains by being transferred to the piano'. Handel's vast *oeuvre* overshadows his small output of harpsichord music to such an extent that neither Paul Henry Lang's *George Frideric Handel* (New York and London, 1966) nor any of its predecessors devotes more than a few pages to the suites, fugues and other pieces.

The study of performance practice, as scholars sometimes term the whole complex of problems we face in realising a composer's intentions, will certainly occupy us for as long as we make music. It would be difficult to think of a better way to begin one's study than reading Thurston Dart's *The Interpretation of Music* (London, 1954), a book which in less than two hundred pages sets forth the basic fundamentals of performance practice from the Middle Ages until the late eighteenth century. Those in search of fuller explanations will find them in Robert Donington's *The Interpretation of Early Music* (London, 1963, rev. ed. 1965), which deals with virtually every conceivable difficulty that might confront the player. The bibliography is not only full but utterly frank, offering sensible evaluations and occasionally well-merited words of caution. The most useful index of ornament symbols is derived from the one prepared by Donington for *Grove's Dictionary of Music and Musicians* (5th ed. by Eric Blom, London and New York, 1954), which also contains excellent articles on the harpsichord, harpsichord playing, baroque interpretation, notation, ornaments and ornamentation, and many other topics by leading authorities.

Arnold Dolmetsch was an authentic genius and one of the pioneers in the revival of interest in the harpsichord and other instruments for playing 'antient musick'. His book *The Interpretation of the Music of the XVIIth and XVIIIth Centuries Revealed by Contemporary Evidence* (London, 1915, corrected edition 1944) is still not superseded by later writings in any fundamental sense. Dolmetsch also published an Appendix containing *Twenty-two Illustrative Pieces* (London, n.d.) which are mainly for keyboard and can be used as practical learning material for applying the principles expounded in his book.

At least three of the eighteenth-century treatises deserve mention here. François Couperin's *L'Art de Toucher le Clavecin* (1716–17) (edited and translated into German by Anna Linde, with an English translation by Mevanwy Williams, Leipzig, 1933), although brief, almost fragmentary in style, is a precious document of genuine practical value to any harpsichordist. Moreover, it contains Couperin's little allemande and eight preludes which are delightful to play. C. P. E. Bach's *Essay on the True Art of Playing Keyboard Instruments* (1753) (translated and edited by William J. Mitchell, New York and London, 1949) errs rather in the direction of excessive length but contains indispensable information about fingering, ornaments, free ornamentation and figured-bass playing. Bach's colleague at the court of Frederick the Great, Johann Joachim Quantz, wrote a lengthy treatise *On Playing the Flute* (1752) (edited and translated by Edward R. Reilly, London, 1966) which is far more than a mere flute method, and in fact a detailed exposition of how music of all types was performed in the mid-eighteenth century.

Practical guidance in the art of realising figured basses is offered by Hermann Keller's *Thoroughbass Method* (translated by Carl Parrish, New York and London, 1967), drawing on the German and Italian repertoire for illustrative material. (Other books, notably

Mellers' *Couperin*, will adequately fill in the missing French links once Keller's method has been mastered.) An encyclopaedic survey of the subject, giving copious extracts from the original source materials, will be found in Peter Williams' *Figured Bass Accompaniment* (Edinburgh, 1970).

Not too many years ago a 'good' edition of a piece of older music (no longer the subject of copyright protection) was considered to be one where a more or less renowned performer or pedagogue had committed his interpretation of the work to paper in the most minute detail. Each note was surmounted by a fingering and an articulation sign, every bar contained some dynamic indication, phrasings were marked with slurs, numerals and other more cabbalistic symbols; in short, the composer's original had become unrecognisable under the accretions of later editorial hands. Worst of all, ornaments were usually misrepresented either by erroneous symbols or incorrect realisations.

Today we have come full circle. We now consider a good edition to be one which, first and foremost, sets down the composer's text clearly, accurately and faithfully. It does not try to solve in advance and thus dictate solutions of every problem to the player. Editorial additions are minimal and clearly recognisable as such. Whatever explanation is required in the editor's judgment for proper performance of the music is set forth in a preface or appendix, and never mixed-in with the musical text itself.

In a few years' time the older type of edition will have disappeared, we hope. At the moment one must still be on one's guard. Even complete editions of the works of the most famous composers are not always to be relied upon, as witness Longo's edition of Scarlatti, its pages cluttered, even disfigured, by a heavy editorial hand which also has bowdlerised harmonies, altered ornaments, and generally dealt far too freely with the original. Kirkpatrick's model edition of sixty sonatas (New York, 1953) and the excellent one by Keller and Weissmann of a hundred and fifty sonatas (Leipzig, 1957) still leave us with only the inaccurate Longo text for more than three hundred sonatas until the appearance of Gilbert's new *Urtext* edition of all five hundred and fifty-five sonatas.

At the start, the harpsichordist will do well to look into a few of the better anthologies so as to gain familiarity with the literature and the various national styles. Fortunately a series of superb volumes have been appearing under the editorship of Howard Ferguson which answer the need in every sense. To date, the following have been published (all in London and New York, 1963 *ff.*):

Style and Interpretation: in the four volumes, the first two deal with harpsichord music; Vol. I, *Early Keyboard Music (I), England and France*, and Vol. II, *Early Keyboard Music (II), Germany and Italy*.
Early French Keyboard Music—an Anthology, 2 vols.
Early Italian Keyboard Music—an Anthology, 2 vols.
Early German Keyboard Music—an Anthology, 2 vols.
Early English Keyboard Music—an Anthology, 2 vols.

Ferguson's meaty introductions give clear and correct instruction on the stylish performance of the music, covering such topics as ornaments and rhythmical alterations in considerable detail. The technical level of the music varies from the most elementary to such advanced virtuoso pieces as Rameau's *Les Cyclopes*.

Other well edited anthologies of early keyboard music include Walter Georgii's *Keyboard Music of the Baroque and Rococo* (3 vols.) (Cologne, 1960), and Hermann Keller's *Alte Meister der Klaviermusik* (4 vols.) (Leipzig, n.d.). The earliest keyboard music, from about 1350 to 1650, is anthologised in Willi Apel's *Musik aus früher Zeit* (2 vols.) (Mainz, 1934).

While certain of the newer publishers such as Henle and Bärenreiter have built their reputations on putting out impeccable pure text editions, many older firms have in fact done their share to replace faulty earlier ones. Unfortunately, having put out, say, an excellent Scarlatti edition by Kirkpatrick or Keller and Weiss-mann, a publisher may not trouble to withdraw the over-edited and inaccurate one by Sauer or Buonamici. Thus one must be chary of thinking solely in terms of music publishers in this regard. In general, the more recent editions of older music tend to present a pure text without excessive editing.

One should soon become familiar with series of good publications, such as Stainer & Bell's excellent printings of British and other early keyboard music: complete works in some cases, selections of works by particular composers, and contemporary anthologies in others. Heugel has recently launched a fine series of publications, *Le Pupitre*, which already includes the complete harpsichord music of François Couperin in the best modern edition, and the works of such lesser masters as Dagincour, Duphly and Forqueray, and has begun to issue a new complete edition of Domenico Scarlatti. A long-felt need for generous and comprehensive selections from the works of many important earlier composers such as Sweelinck and Froberger has still not been met. Schott's *Werkreihe* series, while conservatively edited, offers only scanty selections from the works of the important northern European composers of harpsichord music.

One of the many virtues of the Howard Ferguson anthologies is that they include complete information about the original sources and authoritative modern editions of each composer's works. There is no substitute for browsing through the actual printed notes, learning to distinguish the look of Couperin from Couperin-Diémer, Scarlatti from Scarlatti-Longo, and Bach from Bach-Czerny. Seeking out the true text is an essential step towards achieving an artistic performance.

For further recommended editions of harpsichord music, see page 215.

Appendix
BASIC HARPSICHORD MAINTENANCE

Harpsichords do not show the same stability as modern pianos. There is no evading this fact. And the shortage of qualified harpsichord technicians is particularly acute. In acquiring a harpsichord one thus assumes an inescapable burden of maintenance.

Tuning is the principal recurrent labour. It may be required in a matter of hours if weather conditions change abruptly. With stable humidity and temperature, a tuning can last for weeks. Detailed instructions for tuning appear further on in this appendix.

Stability of regulation and voicing, too, will vary with each instrument as well as with the climate. Variations of detail in design make it impractical to do more than list the minor adjustments which every owner should learn to make, preferably from the builder himself. These are: regulating jacks which sound too early or too late; regulating tongues and plectra for evenness of tone; cutting new and trimming old plectra; regulating entire registers to sound louder or softer; regulating pedals, knee-levers and hand-stops; adjusting or replacing dampers and buff pads; and keeping jacks and tongues working smoothly.

Such are the principal maintenance operations in which the owner is most likely to be involved from time to time. An occasional broken string, fortunately rather a rare occurrence except with instruments improperly strung to begin with, really comes under the heading of repairs but one should know how to replace a broken string if it should become necessary. Probably nothing more serious should ever be attempted except by a technician or, best of all, the builder.

A stringing list may usually be had on request from the builder. This will give the diameters of the steel and brass wire used for particular strings from one end of the compass to the other and for each register. If there are wound strings, these will have to be ordered from the builder or some other qualified supplier. There are two difficulties connected with string replacement. One is that the little loop at the hitch-pin end of the string is difficult to make unless one has a special tool for the purpose. The other is that brass wire becomes brittle when not kept under tension, as it is in the instrument, so that a stock of wires of different sizes kept for a prolonged period may be found to be of little practical worth when the time comes to dip into it and replace a broken brass string. But steel music wire can be kept indefinitely unless it rusts.

Maintenance problems can be minimised by observing a few simple precautions. The harpsichord should be placed against an inside wall or stand free in the room, provided it is not thereby exposed to constant draughts. It should never be placed against an outside wall, especially in damp climates, or near a window where currents of air and the rays of the sun may harm it. Excessive central heating and its attendant dry atmosphere can have lethal effects on harpsichords, leading not only to constant tuning but ultimately to the splitting of the soundboard and perhaps other wooden members, even the wrest-plank in extreme cases. A room humidifier is virtually essential in many centrally-heated homes. By keeping a relative humidity of 40% or more in the room where the harpsichord stands, one will greatly reduce the need to tune and regulate it during the winter months. In very damp summer weather, air-conditioning—provided it is not excessive—will help to achieve the same result. Dehumidifiers can also be of help where excessive humidity without high temperatures is the troublesome atmospheric condition. Essentially those conditions that make for human good health and well-being will do the same for harpsichords.

Tuning is usually carried out by ear, taking the original pitch from a tuning fork, next setting a temperament on one register (usually the upper or front 8-foot) and tuning the whole register, first down to the bass, then up to the treble from the respective ends of the temperament section.

Setting a temperament, that is, filling in the other eleven notes of the chromatic scale in the centre section of the keyboard, requires considerable practice. Some players have found it helpful to purchase not one fork but a set of a dozen, one for each note of the scale. Even more handy but substantially more expensive are electronic tuning devices, such as the Conn Strobotuner, which show with exquisite precision the slightest deviation from exact pitch of any note of the equal-tempered chromatic scale in any octave. Not only can one tune well from the start with such an apparatus at hand, but also under very adverse conditions such as are often encountered in a hall shortly before the performance.

Various methods for tuning in equal temperament have been evolved. That is the system universally employed today in which the octave is divided into twelve equal semi-tones. We present two widely-used versions of temperament patterns, one based on the use of an A-440 tuning fork, and the other on that of a C-523.3 fork, the two forks most commonly used. Actually, by simple transposition of the patterns, one can adapt either pattern to use with any type of fork.

In order to tune, one also needs a tuning hammer, either of the T-hammer or gooseneck types, designed to fit the smaller 'zither' tuning pins used in harpsichords. Since the registers can be engaged or disengaged by stops or pedals, no wedges or mutes are needed for tuning.

Would that all makers would adopt the very logical method used by the old French builders who set out each row of tuning pins grouped to correspond to the arrangement of the keyboard, i.e. with the pins for the sharps set slightly behind those for the naturals.

Certain other makers, who prefer to arrange their tuning pins in straight lines, achieve a similar result by using nickelled pins for the naturals and blued ones for the sharps. If your harpsichord has the usual pins of one type only arranged in a row, then you might do well to mark two in every octave: *D* and *A* if you tune from an A fork, *F* and *C* if you use a C fork. Little felt or paper washers, red or red and blue, can be slipped over the pins. Small dabs of nail lacquer will even serve—but mind that none drips down to the wrest-plank! With multi-register instruments it is usually quite clear which rows of pins affect which strings, but until one is very familiar with the arrangement, it is best to verify it again before each tuning.

The tuning hammer must be firmly placed on the wrest pin, well seated so as to turn the pin gently. The hammer must not rock, or twist it, for that would damage the pin or the wrest-plank and would certainly yield an unstable tuning. This is vital since, for all one's skill in hearing intervals and beats, the proper manipulation of the hammer and wrest pin is essential in bringing the string to the correct pitch and keeping it there. Always begin by tuning the note down slightly. This will prevent one breaking a string if one has accidentally alighted on the wrong pin. Then gently, firmly turn the pin until the proper pitch has been reached.

Next follow the two tuning patterns presented. In each case, the white notes indicate the notes to be tuned and the black notes the tests for accuracy of tuning. No harm will be done by playing additional test notes other than those shown in the pattern. A good choice is the major third below, the major sixth below and the fifth below the note. If all three sound correct, the note is indeed well tuned. But the tests only begin at the seventh note tuned in each pattern and much can go awry before then. If that proves to be the case, it is far wiser to begin all over again than persist in a temperament which is bound to work out badly.

Pattern 1 begins by setting *a'* from the tuning fork. One next tunes the octave below to the first note. This octave must be pure and beatless, as if each component sound were contained in the other. Returning then to the first note, one tunes down a perfect fifth, again trying for a beatless, pure sound like that of two properly-tuned violin strings. When the pure fifth has been tuned, raise the *d'* ever so slightly to temper the fifth, i.e. to narrow it. Continue by another such fifth down to *g*, then up a perfect octave to *g'*, down a tempered fifth to *c'*, and so on to the end. At *f*, step 7, begin to test as shown.

Pattern 1 has the virtue of simplicity, involving only perfect octaves and tempered fifths, and is favoured by continental tuners. It spans a diminished twelfth and lies a bit higher on the keyboard where the beats are more rapid. Therefore many prefer to tune with

Pattern 1

fork

1 2 3 4 5 6 7 i 8

9 ii 10 11 . iii 12 iv 13 14 v

15 vi 16 17 vii 18 19 viii

notes tuned

Pattern 2 which covers only a major ninth (the fork note, c'', lies outside the temperament). However, it requires tuning tempered fourths as well as the perfect octaves and tempered fifths of Pattern 1. Tempered fourths are wider than perfect while tempered fifths are narrower. However, because of the layout of the pattern, tempering both fifths and fourths in Pattern 2 only requires lowering each note tuned from a perfect beatless interval to a tempered one in relation to the previous note tuned.

After completing the setting of the temperament on the first register to be tuned, finish by tuning in octaves down to the bottom and up to the top. Then bring the other 8-foot register into unison with the first one tuned. As a rule, unisons are easier to tune than octaves; the coincidence of the notes is easier to detect than the coincidence of the first partial of the lower note of an octave with the fundamental of the upper note. When both 8-foot registers are in tune, then the 16-foot and the 4-foot are tuned to them in that

order. Major thirds and tenths will serve as checks on the accuracy
of all the tuning beyond the temperament.

  Do not be discouraged if the results of your initial efforts at tuning
sound less than perfect and do not last. An instrument can often be
restored to a relatively good state after its tuning has 'faded' without
doing the entire job afresh. As a rule the first 8-foot register tuned
can be taken as a standard and the others brought back into line
with it. The 4-foot register is usually the one most susceptible to
going out of tune, especially at the upper end, and should be checked
and corrected most frequently of all. Indeed, it is the extremes of
the compass which tend to wander soonest and furthest from the
original tuning. If the centre two or so octaves of the upper or front
8-foot have remained stable, there is still a good possibility of bringing the instrument back into tune without returning to the fork
and the temperament.

  When the instrument must be left untouched for a prolonged

Pattern 2

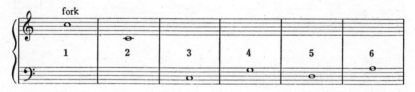

period or shipped far away, it is well to tune it down about a semitone beforehand, to prevent any strain that might result from a sudden drastic change in temperature and humidity. Such a tuned-down harpsichord will require a few tunings before it reaches its normal level of stability, but not so many as a brand-new or freshly restrung instrument. If a harpsichord cannot, in spite of all, be brought up to pitch and kept there for a reasonable period of time, there are grounds for suspecting that some serious damage may have occurred, and the builder or another source of expert help should be consulted forthwith.

SOME RECOMMENDED
EDITIONS OF HARPSICHORD MUSIC

J. S. Bach
    Keyboard Works — Henle, ed. Steglich, Dadelsen and Rönnau
    Keyboard Works — Peters, ed. Landshoff, Soldan, Kreutz and Keller
    Goldberg Variations — Schirmer, ed. Kirkpatrick

Cabezón
    Selected Keyboard Works (2 vols.) — Schott, ed. Kastner

François Couperin
    Pièces de Clavecin (4 vols.) — Heugel, ed. Gilbert
    Selected Harpsichord Music — Schirmer, ed. Marlowe

Louis Couperin
    Pièces de Clavecin — Heugel, ed. Curtis

Frescobaldi
    Keyboard Works (5 vols.) — Bärenreiter, ed. Pidoux

Froberger
    Selected Works — Peters, ed. Schultz
    Selected Keyboard Works — Schott, ed. Schubert
    6 Suites — Bosworth, ed. Frickert

Handel
    Keyboard Works (4 vols.) — Bärenreiter, ed. Steglich, Northway and Best
    Keyboard Works (5 vols.) — Peters, ed. Serauky and von Glasenapp

Purcell
    Complete Keyboard Works (2 vols.) — Stainer and Bell, ed. Ferguson

Rameau
    Pièces de Clavecin — Bärenreiter, ed. Jacobi

Domenico Scarlatti

Complete Sonatas (11 vols.)	Heugel, ed. Gilbert
60 Sonatas (2 vols.)	Schirmer, ed. Kirkpatrick
150 Sonatas (3 vols.)	Peters, ed. Keller and Weissmann

Sweelinck

Keyboard Works, vol. I, part III (1968)	Vereniging voor Nederlandse Muziekgeschiednis, ed. Noske
Liedvariationen	Schott, ed. Doflein

Virginalists

Parthenia	Stainer and Bell, ed. Dart
Fitzwilliam Virginal Book (2 vols.)	Dover (reprint edition), ed. Fuller-Maitland and Barclay-Squire
Selected Keyboard Works of Bull, Byrd, Farnaby, Gibbons, and others	Stainer and Bell, ed. Dart and others

Anthologies

Ferguson's *Style and Interpretation* and *Early Keyboard Music* volumes are published by the Oxford University Press. The Georgii anthology is published by Arno Volk, the Keller *Alte Meister* collection by Peters, and Apel's *Musik aus früher Zeit* by Schott.

Silva Iberica, two volumes of Spanish and Portuguese keyboard music edited by Kastner (Schott), complements the Ferguson volumes. *A First Harpsichord Book*, edited by Igor Kipnis (Oxford University Press), offers a selection of less demanding pieces with suggestions for fingering and articulation.

INDEX

Page numbers in italics indicate musical examples